WEDDING RITES

WEDDING RITES

A Complete Guide to Traditional Vows, Music,
Ceremonies, Blessings, and Interfaith Services

Michael P. Foley

With

Alexander E. Lessard,

Angela Lessard, &

Alexandra Foley

WILLIAM B. EERDMANS PUBLISHING COMPANY
GRAND RAPIDS, MICHIGAN / CAMBRIDGE, U.K.

Published 2008 by

Wm. B. Eerdmans Publishing Co.

2140 Oak Industrial Drive N.E., Grand Rapids, Michigan 49505 /

P.O. Box 163, Cambridge CB3 9PU U.K.

Printed in the United States of America

14 13 12 11 10 09 08   7 6 5 4 3 2 1

Library of Congress Cataloging-in-Publication Data

Foley, Michael P., 1970-
    Wedding rites: a complete guide to traditional vows, music,
    ceremonies, blessings, and interfaith services / Michael P. Foley;
    with Alexander E. Lessard, Angela Lessard & Alexandra Foley.
        p.   cm.
    Includes bibliographical references and index.
    ISBN 978-0-8028-4867-3 (pbk.: alk. paper)
    1. Marriage — Religious aspects — Christianity.
    2. Marriage — Religious aspects — Judaism.
    3. Marriage customs and rites.   4. Weddings.
    I. Lessard, Alexander E.   II. Lessard, Angela.
    III. Foley, Alexandra.   IV. Title.

BV835.F57   2008
265'.5 — dc22

                                 2008003711

www.eerdmans.com

To Alexandra, my heart's sister

Contents

Acknowledgments

L IKE A GOOD WEDDING, this book has come about with the help of many friends. I especially wish to thank the following: Lawrence LaRose and Ms. Cory Halaby for their judicious practical advice; my former colleagues in the Notre Dame Department of Theology, Rabbi Michael Signer, Prof. Maxwell Johnson, and Prof. Timothy Matovina for their valuable guidance; Notre Dame students Fr. Michael Hutson and Marcela Klicova for their helpful input and work, respectively; and Fr. Thomas R. Dobrowolski and Perry Hamalis for their kind assistance in elucidating the Byzantine Christian tradition.

I also wish to express particular gratitude to Angela Lessard, friend to me and godmother to my Mary, for enriching this book with her tasteful and inspiring musical advice; to my beloved wife Alexandra for her incomparable expertise on flowers and for her unwavering encouragement; and above all to my forever best-man Alex, without whose foundational involvement and keen eye this volume would not be what it is.

A Note on Terms and Texts

THIS BOOK COVERS the great wedding traditions of two of the great Western religions, Judaism and Christianity. Since we are therefore dealing with a religious topic, it is helpful to get our terminology in order.

For ease of reference, this book uses the term *Jewish* to refer to all Jewish believers without distinction to the main branches of modern Judaism: Orthodox, Reform, and Conservative. However, on account of differences in custom, we occasionally distinguish *Ashkenazic* from *Sephardic* Jews. The Ashkenazim are Yiddish-speaking Jews who settled in central and northern Europe, while the Sephardim are the Jews who lived in Spain, Portugal, North Africa, and the Middle East.

This book uses the term *Protestant* to refer to all ecclesial communities that take their bearing from the Protestant Reformation (including those that are nondenominational or Evangelical) or that broke away from the Catholic Church in the sixteenth century, such as the Church of England. The word *Byzantine* refers to all Christians from the Eastern Orthodox and Eastern Catholic churches who worship according to the liturgical traditions of ancient Constantinople. Sometimes we use the phrase *Western Christian,* by which we basically mean Protestants and Roman Catholics (Catholics of the Roman rite) but not Christians of the Byzantine rite. Unfortunately, because of the cruel constraints of space, we have overlooked the Christian churches that are neither Roman nor

Byzantine nor Protestant, such as the Armenian, Chaldean, and Maronite.

Regarding the texts used in this book, all scriptural passages are taken from our family Bible, the Douay-Rheims translation. (You may, however, wish to replace these with texts from your own family or church Bible.) The translations of the Jewish and Byzantine rites of marriage are taken from J. Foote Bingham's *Christian Marriage* (1900). The translation of the Jewish *tenaim* document is taken from Mendell Lewittes' *Jewish Marriage* (Northvale, NJ: Jason Aronson Inc., 1994), while the translation of Martin Luther's marriage service is taken from Ulrich Leupold's *Luther's Works,* vol. 53 (Philadelphia: Fortress Press, 1965). All passages for Presbyterian and Methodist weddings are taken from the 1906 edition of the *Book of Common Worship* and the 1964 edition of the *Book of Worship,* respectively. The translations of virtually all French and Latin texts, on the other hand, are mine. That includes, but is not limited to, the French betrothal rite, the medieval vows and blessings, the Roman solemn nuptial blessing, and all of John Calvin's 1542 marriage service.

In order to remain faithful to both the spirit and the letter, the spellings and conventions of the original liturgical books have been retained as much as possible. Hence the reader will find different spellings for Sarah/Sara, honor/honour, and so on. All rubrical titles, however, have been made consistent with each other. "M." designates the lines of the man (groom), "W." the woman (bride), "N." the proper name to be inserted, "P." the pastor or presider, and "R." the response of the wedding party and congregation.

Preface

O Beauty,
Ever ancient,
Ever new.

St. Augustine,
Confessions X.xxvii

I T IS EASY TO FORGET amidst the countless price-per-slice decisions made in planning a wedding that the most important part of
the most important day in your life is the ceremony itself. Without it,
the great reception that has been planned would be merely another
party; because of it, two people mysteriously become one flesh as they
formally embark on their life's journey together. And if the wedding ceremony defines this sea change in one's life, it is the traditional wedding
which best expresses its new meaning and quality.

Why a traditional wedding? For one thing, because it is beautiful.
The symbols and statements from these ancient rites come from an age
when most could read only gestures, not texts. Actions and spoken
words thus took on a great importance, signifying the mystery of marriage with a humble and direct simplicity. And because the meanings of
these ceremonies were meant to be remembered long after the ceremo-

nies themselves had passed, they were made as stunning and as lovely as possible.

Second, a wedding is not just the hope for a happy future, but a fond reminder of the past. Weddings (and we can attest to this personally) bring out a traditional sense which many people never knew they had. Family traditions — such as a bride wearing her grandmother's necklace or a father offering advice to his son about his new responsibilities — have always added special meaning to a nuptial celebration. And the longer these traditions go back, the more they are cherished. It is as if these simple customs formed a living link to all of our loved ones, past and present. The service itself is no different. When you celebrate a wedding whose fabric has been woven from the thread of tradition, you connect yourself to the generations of lovers who have gone before you and who will come after you, and who all live in Love's eternal memory.

Third, as more and more couples are coming to realize, traditional symbols are of permanent value. Unlike the trends that come and go, they will not render your wedding video or photograph album an embarrassment ten or twenty years from now. This does not mean that your wedding will be boring or predictable. So many traditions have been forgotten that resurrecting them will make your wedding truly original. (In a supreme twist of irony, it is the hot-air-balloon and underwater weddings which have become cliché.) Fortunately, the originality of a traditional wedding comes with virtually no risk: Its customs have been tested and perfected over generations, and thus there is little chance of your wedding looking contrived or dated. And because traditional ceremonies do not cost much or unduly lengthen your service, you will be adding great detail to your wedding without taxing yourselves or your guests.

We came upon the idea for *Wedding Rites* almost by necessity. When Michael started to prepare for his wedding with his fiancée Alexandra, he discovered a surprising gap in the available nuptial literature. While there was a flood of material to help make the right decisions about ribbons and reception lines, the books for the service itself amounted to a trickle. And of these books, none of them comprehensively covered every aspect of the service, despite several claims to the contrary.

Since Michael was earning his doctorate in theology at the time, he decided to do some research of his own. He consulted a number of works on the history of weddings and examined several old service manuals. He was looking for the best and most easily implemented marriage ceremonies, vows, blessings, and customs within the Jewish and Christian traditions. What he discovered far exceeded all of our expectations, both in quality and quantity. We were especially astonished to learn of how many wonderful and perfectly feasible customs remain unknown to engaged couples, wedding planners, and even religious leaders.

Hence this book, which we write for couples, planners, priests, ministers, and rabbis who want to have or to hold a traditional wedding but are uncertain where to turn or which resources to consult. *Wedding Rites* provides a collection of nuptial music, readings, vows, ceremonies, and blessings which are easy to reference and easy to use. The classical nuptial tradition is vast, stretching from the rise of Judaism to the decline of Christendom, and it extends over richly varied cultures and religious communities. That is why you will find within these pages such a wide assortment of options: blessings for a young couple from sixth-century Rome, consummation rites from medieval France, opening allocutions from an infant America. We have even succeeded in retrieving many gems that had been lost, translating a number of prayers and blessings into English for the first time. And to assist you in assimilating the best of these traditions into your own wedding, we offer concrete suggestions at each stage of planning and a special word of advice for each chapter. Finally, we devote the concluding chapter to helping you put it all together.

We wish our readers all the joys and blessings which attend a traditional wedding.

Hobbs Brook
January 23, 2008
Feast of the Espousals
of Mary and Joseph

Mike Foley, *along with*
Alex Lessard,
Angela Lessard &
Alexandra Foley

WEDDING RITES

INTRODUCTION

Having a Traditional Wedding

Happy, thrice happy and more,
Are they whom an unbroken bond unites
And whose love shall know no sundering quarrels
So long as they shall live . . .
With you I should love to live,
With you be ready to die.

Horace,
Odes I.xiii.17 & III.ix.last

A TRADITIONAL WEDDING does not go out of style, take more time and money, or become burdensome to prepare. However, like any other wedding, this is only true if it is well-conceived and well-executed. The couple who wants a successful wedding must do more than simply pick an appropriate ceremony: They must learn how to turn their vision into a concrete reality. We have drafted the following list of guidelines, which come mostly from our own experience with planning weddings but also from our general familiarity with ecclesiastical matters. Bear in mind that this list is not complete — advice from trusted married couples, wedding professionals, and pastors is an important complement to what is mentioned here.

1. **Think grand.**   By this we do not mean the size of the guest list or the scale of the trimmings: The grandeur we have in mind could be present at an intimate and inexpensive wedding. What we are referring to is essentially the willingness to let ritual splendor permeate all the stages of your courtship and wedding, from a solemn betrothal months before your marriage service to a blessing of the loving cup hours after. This requires a different state of mind from the one that usually directs our personal and professional lives. But since your initiation into marriage is, to say the least, something rare and precious, it makes sense to drop the minimalist mind-set this time and to savor the extra details. For example, we recommend looking into a good choir that can sing more advanced music, such as polyphony or chant. Or if there are any decorations in the church which are of questionable taste, we recommend that you remove them before the service and restore them afterwards. In shaping your service, however, do not get carried away by too much pomp. Ritual does not have to be big to be grand.

2. **Speak to your parents, grandparents, and relatives.**   Ask them what they did at their wedding. Family traditions add little hassle to your big day but enrich it immeasurably. A family tradition can be rooted in one's ethnicity (such as having a certain folk dance at the reception), or in the personality of a relative (such as the lovable uncle who wrote a different song for each of his nephews' weddings). More often than not the custom will be simple and sweet — a toast of Sambuca with three coffee beans, or a singing of "Let Me Call You Sweetheart" as the newlyweds depart for their honeymoon.* Whatever it is, we guarantee that this little heirloom of word or gesture will be one of the most vivid memories you and your guests take with you.

3. **Choose your service.**   One of the first things you should do is to decide what kind of service you and your fiancé(e) want. If you are both of the same faith, you should have little difficulty in agreeing on the basic format, which will depend for the most part on your religious affiliation (see Chapter VIII for the basic options). With an outline of your service

---

* All of these examples, incidentally, are from weddings we personally witnessed.

in mind, you can choose the prayers, blessings, and ceremonies which seem most appropriate to you. Make certain, however, to consult first with your rabbi, pastor, or parish wedding planner to determine the parameters of your religious community and to run all of your ideas by him or her at every stage of development. Many religious communities have revised their rites in recent years, and some may not want you to observe a particular custom from the past. Viewing this book as a supplement to current wedding practices is a prudent move for some couples and a practical necessity for others.

If you are of different faiths or denominations, you have three options: (1) two separate weddings (which in some cases is asked of the couple); (2) a wedding in the faith of either the bride or the groom; or (3) a wedding which in some way combines the rites of both parties. This third possibility, while vulnerable to eclecticism, can nevertheless be done well, especially when both parties are Protestant: Since many American denominations traditionally followed the wedding service from the 1790 Episcopalian Book of Prayer, there is a common foundation on which to work. In Chapter VIII we will speak more on how to plan an ecumenical wedding.

4. **Be attentive to your selections.** This book, having been written with you in mind, will give you more than enough options from which to choose. But this does not mean that any combination of prayers will do. Read everything carefully with an eye towards an overall harmony or complementarity of parts. You want your wedding to be a smooth and unified whole, not a conglomerate of disjointed fragments.

5. **Know your presider.** By this we are suggesting that you gain a reasonable knowledge of the priest, rabbi, or minister who will preside at your wedding, and vice versa. The more familiar you are with your presider (and vice versa), the better: You will gain a deeper mutual trust, and your presider will have more things to say about you during the homily or sermon. If your presider does not know you very well, it is a good idea to have dinner together prior to the wedding. And if you have the liberty to be selective, you should select someone whose character or style is compatible with the type of wedding you want. Assuming, for

example, that you want your wedding ceremony to evoke awe and not guffaws, you may wish to avoid the presider who does a stand-up shtick in the sanctuary.

This raises the delicate question of who is ultimately in charge of the wedding. Pastors obviously have authority and *should* have authority over what kind of ceremony takes place at their parish. On the other hand, according to Western Christian theology at least, it is the consent of the couple that makes a marriage a marriage; the presider "solemnizes" the marriage or declares the two man and wife, but the presider does not make them so. This means that the couple should also have at least some input, especially when the presider is being paid for his services. You should always be respectful and tactful, but at the same time you should not be afraid to state your preferences; it is, after all, your wedding. The only reasonable objections we could foresee would be if you were requesting an excessive number of ceremonies or something alien to your faith. But if the custom comes from your own religious tradition, a presider could not question it without also calling into question the whole heritage which he represents. Consequently, we do not anticipate many objections to traditional practices. As a matter of fact, most pastors will be delighted with the age-old elements of your wedding.

6. Divide the labor. Both the bride and groom should decide together what kind of marriage service they want. As a practical rule of thumb, however, we suggest that the groom or perhaps his family be in charge of the preparations. Our reasoning is that the bride's family already has a lot of responsibilities. Preparing a wedding reception, finding the right gown or band, and handling the notification and seating of guests involve a lot of time and work. The groom, on the other hand, generally has fewer tasks and thus more time to take care of the liturgy. Giving the groom this task will also make him more enthusiastic about the service, as he will be able to take personal pride in its success. And we should add that the groom's active participation in the liturgical preparation is, in some places at least, the more traditional arrangement.

7. Start early. You have heard this piece of advice regarding every other part of the wedding; now apply it to the service. Some churches can be booked literally years in advance (one prescient bride we know actually reserved a popular church she wanted *before* her fiancé even proposed). Choirs, either parochial or professional, can have busier schedules than you might expect, and the same goes for presiders. Further, the more you prepare for your marriage service, the more perfect it will be. Gain an early command of the preparations, and you will be pleased with the results.

8. **Practice.**   The key to a smooth wedding is having everyone know exactly what he or she is supposed to do. Presiders should be given a copy of the complete service, with their parts highlighted, as soon as possible; choirs should be told exactly what and when to sing; and the wedding party should have a thorough (though not taxing) rehearsal the night before. Most of all, both bride and groom should know the details of the service well enough to answer any question that any of the participants might have.

9. **Make a program.**   Your guests will be able to enjoy the features of your wedding much more if they can follow them in a program. Programs not only enlighten and inform; they remove the restlessness that comes from being confused or lost during an unfamiliar service. This does not mean that every word of the service must be transcribed, but it would, for example, be helpful to have an outline of the order or a brief description of an unusual custom which you have included (see Chapter VIII). Finally, the program can be one more item of beauty to enrich the nuptial experience. With the right font, stationery, and attention to detail, your program can be a lasting keepsake for a memorable day.

I. Sealing the Engagement: Betrothals and Banns

Now go with me and with this holy man
Into the chantry by; there, before him,
And underneath that consecrated roof,
Plight me the full assurance of your faith;
That my most jealous and too doubtful soul
May live at peace.

Shakespeare,
Twelfth Night IV.iii.23-28

MARRIAGE IS A BIG STEP, which is why it was traditionally preceded by smaller ones. A progressive series of rituals and customs helped ease young lovers in their transition from singlehood to married life. We would like to introduce you to two of these customs: solemn betrothals and the reading of the banns.

Traditionally, the first thing to happen after the couple agreed to marry would be a betrothal ceremony. Though many of us may have never heard of them before, solemn betrothals were common in Europe and the Middle East long before the birth of Christianity, and they continue to be used by several communities today. The vows of a solemn betrothal are generally less binding than those of a marriage but more momentous than a simple pledge. In other words, they seal the engagement proposal and better prepare the couple for their final vows.

After a couple had solemnly promised to marry, they would have the banns read at their church. This ancient Christian custom is an announcement to the whole parish of their intentions. Though also somewhat of a rarity today, the reading of the banns was practiced by nearly all churches until about a generation ago.

Together or separately, these practices not only help bridge the gap between being two separate people and becoming one flesh, but they also reassure the couple of each other's faith and confirm them in their decision. To paraphrase Olivia's remark to her fiancé Sebastian in *Twelfth Night,* they help an understandably nervous soul live in peace until the big day.

In this chapter we will present a number of betrothal rites and banns. We will point out which of them are the most feasible, and we will offer some general suggestions on how to go about planning them.

Betrothal, or "Handfasting"

The solemn betrothal officially initiates a couple into a higher and more meaningful phase of their courtship.* Like the wedding itself, betrothals have both a serious and a joyous side. On the serious side there is not only the formal affirmation of proposal and acceptance but a "plighting of one's troth," a solemn promise to marry. (There is a difference between proposing marriage [engagement] and promising to go through with that proposal [betrothal].) In the Latin West, that promise was not as binding as a marital vow (it could be broken if there were good reason), but keeping it under normal circumstances was nonetheless viewed as a grave moral responsibility. And there were other obligations that went with it, all of which were eminently reasonable and some of which were

---

* In some places, such as Argentina, betrothals even serve as the traditional occasion for the exchange of *wedding* rings. In Chile, on the other hand, the couple traditionally wear their rings on their right hand after the betrothal and switch them to the left hand after the exchange of their wedding vows.

mildly amusing. After a betrothal, it became one's *duty* to engage in "customary signs of affection" such as non-lascivious or "honorable" kissing and conversation; nor could fiancés "render themselves unfit for marriage" through self-imposed impotency or voluntarily contracting "any notable defect that would make them in a marked degree less desirable as husband and wife"!* (Would that include body-piercing?) Finally, in the Catholic Church, just as marriage was understood to be a sacrament (a divinely established channel of grace), betrothal was valued as its "sacramental," something that helps one better prepare for the reception of a sacrament.

On the joyous side, solemn betrothals are a wonderful way of sharing your exuberance at getting engaged. They are especially nice to have if you are planning a large wedding because they give you an intimacy with your friends and family that a large wedding lacks. There is also a greater flexibility with betrothals: Unlike a traditional wedding, which usually takes place in church, a traditional "handfasting" can take place at one's home.

Michael and his then-fiancée Alexandra had a solemn betrothal from a medieval French rite (see below) in a beautiful little chapel filled with twenty-five of their family and friends. After the ceremony Alexandra's parents held a cocktails-and-hors-d'oeuvre reception at their house, where many of the couple's acquaintances got to know each other for the first time. Michael and Alexandra loved the whole affair, both for the reasons mentioned above and for a practical motive: It gave them a good foretaste of what it would be like to make vows in front of others, and therefore made them more confident at their wedding several months later.

It is little wonder, then, that betrothals have been making a minor comeback in the last several years. The 1989 U.S. Catholic *Book of Blessings* contains an "Order for the Blessing of an Engaged Couple" which, while technically not a betrothal (no promises are made), reflects the hunger for pre-marital "liturgical way stations." Similarly, several Catholic pre-Cana programs and even colleges have been returning to genuine betrothals within the past two decades. Nor is this renewal limited to

---

* Alöis de Smet, *Betrothment and Marriage* (St. Louis, MO: B. Herder Book Co., 1912), 21-22.

Roman Catholic circles, as the 1980s resurgence of betrothals in the Episcopalian Church attests, as well as the rite of betrothal promulgated at the turn of the new millennium by the United Methodists and Congregationalists. To supplement these recent editions, we include here several classic betrothals.

A SHAKESPEAREAN BETROTHAL

This charming betrothal takes place in Act IV of *Winter's Tale* and is a good model for a simple and intimate ceremony in one's home. Instead of a pastor, both fathers of the couple ask the questions and make the official proclamation of the engagement. Perhaps besides the clasp of hands some symbolic action, such as a kiss or drinking from the same cup, could be added to enrich the event further. If the cup is chosen, one of the fathers could adapt a blessing of the loving cup to the occasion (see Chapter VII). The rite dramatized in the following passage is not difficult to do, though we suspect that only the most thespian of couples will want to repeat it verbatim. In any case, the language can be simplified if an in-home betrothal is what you desire.

Groom's Father: Let me hear what you profess.

Groom: Were I crown'd the most imperial monarch,
                  Thereof most worthy, were I the fairest youth
                  That ever made eye swerve, had force and knowledge
                  More than was ever man's, I would not prize them
                  Without her love: for her employ them all;
                  Commend them and condemn them to her service
                  Or to their own perdition.

Bride's Father: My daughter, say you the like to him?

Bride: I cannot speak so well, nothing so well,
                  no, nor mean better:
                  [But] by the pattern of mine thoughts I cut out
                  The purity of his.

Bride's Father:	Take hands; a bargain;
	And, friends, you shall bear witness to't:
	I give my daughter to him,
	And will make her portion equal his.

They join hands.

Groom:	I take thy hand; this hand,
	As soft as dove's down, and as white as it,
	Or Ethiopian's tooth, or the fann'd snow
	That's bolted by the northern blasts twice o'er.

A French Solemn Betrothal Rite

Even though solemn betrothals were familiar to Christians in the West from the earliest times up until the 1600s, they were especially popular in France, which retained the custom all the way into the twentieth century. The following is actually a compilation of three French rites: one from the twelfth century, one from the thirteenth, and one from the nineteenth. The service is not difficult to implement because of its similarity to the marriage rite and for this very reason is good practice for a wedding. It can be held by itself or immediately before a church service such as the Mass.

> *At church before the altar. At hand are the missal, the holy water, and the engagement ring. The priest (P) enters the sanctuary, accompanied by an altar server. He proceeds to the front of the sanctuary, where he waits for the man (M) and the woman (W) who, with the witnesses, come forward at this time. The priest addresses them in these words:*

P. The betrothal ceremony, which since ancient times has constantly preceded the celebration of marriage, is entirely distinct from the sacrament you intend to receive. It is a simple promise that Christians who wish to be united by marriage make to each other in the presence of the Church, before being irrevocably joined together. The union into which you will enter is so holy — and the things which follow from it so important — that the Church does not receive your pledges except by degrees, so to speak, and she wants to be assured of your whole will before blessing and consecrating your vows. Such is the goal of Christian betrothal; and if we bless in the Lord's name these simple promises, it is to bring your hearts better disposed to the most excellent grace of the sacrament.

The priest then inquires into their intentions:

P. N., do you wish to take N., who is present here, as your wife and spouse, if Holy Church consents?

M. I do.

P. N., do you wish to take N., who is present here, as your husband and spouse, if Holy Church consents?

W. I do.

P. Then let us receive, in the name of the Church, your mutual promises which will be fulfilled at the moment you receive the sacrament of marriage.

The priest instructs the couple to join their right hands, his over hers, and asks each in their turn to repeat after him:

M. I, N., affirm with my mouth, pledge by the faith of my heart, and swear by my baptism and by my Christianity, that I will take thee, N., as wife and as spouse in _____ months' time.

W. I, N., affirm with my mouth, pledge by the faith of my heart, and swear by my baptism and by my Christianity, that I will take thee, N., as husband and as spouse in _____ months' time.

The priest then takes the two ends of his stole and in the form of a cross places them over the clasped hands of the couple. Holding the stole in place with his left hand, he says:

I bear witness of your solemn proposal and I declare you betrothed. May what has begun in you be brought to perfection, for the honor of God and of Our Lady and of all the Saints. In the name of the Father and of the Son and of the Holy Spirit. Amen.

Next, the ring is blessed.

P. The Lord be with you.

R. And with thy spirit.

P. Let us pray.

Creator and Preserver of mankind, Giver of spiritual grace, Bestower of eternal salvation: Send Thou, O Lord, Thy Spirit the Paraclete upon this ring, that she who wears it may be armed with the strength of a heavenly defense, and may it profit her unto eternal salvation. Through Christ our Lord. Amen.

He sprinkles the ring with holy water.

The man now places the ring first on the woman's index finger, then on the middle finger, and then on the lady finger, saying:

In the name of the Father, and of the Son, ✠ and of the Holy Spirit. Amen.

The priest opens the missal to the beginning of the canon and allows the man, and then the woman, to kiss the illustration of the crucifixion.*

THE BYZANTINE BETROTHAL

This rite, dating from the early Middle Ages, reflects all the jubilance of the Byzantine liturgy, with its ornate symbolism and nuanced prayers. It is still used today in Eastern Orthodox churches and in the Eastern Catholic churches which celebrate the Byzantine rite.

After Holy Communion, the couple and two attendants present themselves in front of the Iconostasis (the altar screen of a Byzantine church). A censor, two candles, and two rings (one gold and one silver) are at hand.

---

* Modern Catholic sacramentaries, or "missals," no longer have an illustration of the crucifixion at the beginning of the Eucharistic prayers. Couples may wish to use a crucifix, Bible, or icon instead.

The priest (P) makes the sign of the cross over the heads of the couple three times and gives them the two lit candles. Then, after bringing them into the sanctuary, he incenses them in the form of the cross. Next, the priest, deacon (D), and choir or congregation (R) chant a series of prayers asking for the Lord's mercy. When they are done, the priest says:

O eternal God, who dost bring together into unity things that are divided, ordaining the bond of a covenant not to be broken; Thou who didst bless Isaac and Rebecca, and appoint them heirs of Thy promise: Do Thou bless also these Thy servants, guiding them in every good work.

For Thou art a God of mercy and loving-kindness, and to Thee we ascribe the glory: the Father and the Son and the Holy Spirit, now and always, for ever and ever.

R.   Amen.

P.   Peace be to all.

D.   Let us bow our heads to the Lord.

P.   O Lord our God, who didst pre-engage to Thyself from the nations Thy holy, virgin Church, bless these engagements and unite and keep these Thy servants in peace and harmony. For to Thee is due all glory and honor and worship: the Father and the Son and the Holy Spirit, now and always, for ever and ever.

R.   Amen.

The priest takes the gold ring and gives it to the man, saying to him three times:

The servant of God, N., engages to himself the handmaid of God, N., in the name of the Father, and of the Son, ✠ and of the Holy Spirit. Amen.

He makes the sign of the cross on his head with the ring, and sets it on the forefinger of his right hand.

Then the priest takes the silver ring and gives it to the woman, saying to her three times:

The handmaid of God, N., engages to herself the servant of God, N., in the name of the Father and of the Son ✠ and of the Holy Spirit. Amen.

He makes the sign of the cross on her head with the ring, and sets it on the forefinger of her right hand.

The attendants of the couple then exchange the rings of the newly be-trothed for them.

Next, the priest makes the following prayer over the couple and the rings:

Of the Lord let us make entreaty.

O Lord our God, who didst go with the servant of the patri-arch Abraham in Mesopotamia, sent to betroth for his master Isaac a wife, and by means of drawing water didst disclose that Rebecca should be engaged: Do Thou bless the engagement of Thy servants, this N. here present and this N. here present, and establish the word which has been spoken between them. Confirm them in that holy oneness which is of Thee; for Thou didst from the beginning create male and female, and of Thee is woman joined to man, for helpfulness and a succession of the human race.

Do Thou, therefore, O Lord our God, who didst send forth the truth upon Thine inheritance and Thy promise upon Thy servants our fathers, Thy chosen from generation to generation, look upon Thy servant, this N. here present, and Thy handmaid, this N. here present, and establish their engagement in trust and like-mindedness and truth and love.

For Thou, O Lord, hast shown us that the engagement-pledge should be given and established in every way. By a ring was the power given to Joseph in Egypt; by a ring was Daniel glorified in the land of Babylon; by a ring was Tamar's truthfulness manifested; by a ring our heavenly Father was merciful toward the prodigal son, for he says, "Put a ring on his hand, and bring hither the fatted calf, and kill it; and let us eat and be merry." Thine own right hand itself, O Lord, encamped Moses in the Red Sea; for by Thine own true word the heavens were established and the foundations of Thy servants also shall be blessed by Thy mighty word and by Thy uplifted arm. Do Thou, then, also now Thyself, O Sovereign Master, bless this setting of rings with Thy heavenly blessing: and may the Angel of the Lord go on before them all the days of their life.

For Thou art He who dost bless and sanctify all things, and to Thee we ascribe the glory: the Father and the Son and the Holy Spirit, now and always, for ever and ever. Amen.

Some churches that practice the Byzantine rite end the service here. Others conclude with the following:

D. Let us say from our whole soul, and from our whole mind let us say.

R. Lord, have mercy.

D. O Lord Almighty, God of our fathers, we pray Thee hear and have mercy.

R. Lord, have mercy.

D. Have mercy upon us, O God, according to Thy great mercy, hear and have mercy.

R. Lord, have mercy.

D. Moreover, we pray for mercy, life, peace, health, safety, watchful care, pardon, and remission of sins of the servants of God, this N. here present, and this N. here present, who have now engaged themselves to one another.

R. For Thou art a God of mercy and loving-kindness, and to Thee we ascribe the glory: the Father and the Son and the Holy Spirit, now and always, for ever and ever. Amen.

The choir then chants Psalm 34:1-10. When they are done, the priest faces the congregation and says:

P. The blessing of the Lord, and His mercy come upon us, by His grace and loving-kindness, at all times, now and always, for ever and ever.

R. Amen.

An Olde German Betrothal

This simple rite found in a 1543 manual from Metz was originally designed to be a church ceremony led by a priest, but it can be adapted to any number of settings, from an event held at home to a larger liturgical celebration that includes other ceremonials such as a ring blessing. We also like this rite because it puts the man through his paces and makes him do all the talking, just as with the proposal.

The priest (or presider) asks the man to repeat:

M. I, N., promise to take thee, N., for my lady and my wife; and I promise by the faith of my body to marry you in the presence of our Holy Mother Church in _____ weeks if God and our Holy Mother Church consent to it.

P. Lady, you have heard the promises that N. has made: do you promise to him the same?

W. I do.

P. Then I engage you. May what has begun in you be brought to perfection in the name of the Father and of the Son ✠ and of the Holy Spirit. Amen.

A Jewish *Tenaim*

Originally the Jewish betrothal, like its Christian and pagan counterparts, was as important as the wedding itself. After a solemn pledge to marry had been made and a gift given, the couple was considered virtually married. All that remained was the wedding feast which followed the ritual procession of the bride from her parents' home to her new husband's.

Eventually, however, the betrothal ceremony *(kiddushin)* was combined with the nuptials to the point that now it is not a separate event but the first part of a Jewish wedding. Though it is still technically possible to have a separate *kiddushin,* it would make one's status under

Jewish law rather complicated and would mark a confusing break from recent tradition. Instead we recommend an old Ashkenazic custom for the Jewish couple desirous of a ritual acknowledgment of their engagement. *Tenaim* — literally, the "conditions" of marriage — is a prenuptial agreement which goes back to the twelfth century and which is in some circles making a strong comeback. This ceremony is a formal announcement of a couple's intention to marry and the conditions upon which they agree to do so. The contract stipulating these conditions (also called *tenaim*) includes such factors as the dowry, the date and time of the wedding, and a *knas,* or penalty, if either party fails to fulfill his or her end of the deal. After the *tenaim* is read aloud and signed, a plate or a piece of crockery is smashed, a gesture which both recalls the destruction of the Temple and anticipates the smashing of the glass cup at the wedding. It is also customary at these events to have a *kinyan,* a pledging of some object (perhaps an engagement ring?) to seal the agreement.

Tenaim ceremonies are wonderful ways of not only sharing your joy with friends and relatives, but of beginning your wedding preparations in an appropriately Jewish manner. They also have the great practical advantage of helping the couple make known to each other, concretely and specifically, what each expects out of the marriage. *Tenaim* documents should therefore be crafted with care.

Because of its simplicity, *tenaim* is more flexible in its implementation than a wedding. It does not require any official presider and can be coordinated with any number of engagement parties and social functions. Or if you prefer, the document can simply be signed privately and shown to no one.

We include a copy of a traditional *tenaim* contract, but bear in mind that this tradition has not been codified by Jewish law. Accordingly, there is greater liberty to draft your document in a way that includes your own hopes and expectations. Also, you can have it penned in virtually any format you want: Hebrew or English, calligraphed or handwritten, etc.

Mazel Tov!*

May it rise and sprout like a watered garden;
May God, who is good, pronounce the union good.
Who so findeth a wife findeth a good thing, and obtaineth favor
    of the Lord.
Who declareth the end from the beginning,
May He give a good name and a remainder.

To these words of condition and covenant spoken and stipulated between these two parties: On the one part Mr. N. of [city of residence], who stands on behalf of his son the groom N.; and on the second part Mr. N. of [city of residence], who stands on behalf of his daughter the bride, the maiden N.

First of all, the aforementioned groom will marry for mazel tov the aforementioned bride in a betrothal and *chuppah* according to the law of Moses and Israel; and they shall neither sequester nor conceal one from the other any sums of money wherever held, but shall control them in equal portions; they shall live together in peace, love, brotherhood, and companionship for the length of many days. We asked her and she said yes.

    The aforementioned Mr. N. obligates himself to provide for his son the agreed-upon sum in cash and in raiment for the Sabbath and Festivals and weekdays as befits his honor and corresponding to the value of the dowry gifts to the bride. Mr. N. obligates himself to give his daughter the bride a dowry, the value of which was agreed upon, also alimentary support for the young couple as agreed upon, in cash and in raiment for the Sabbath and Festivals and weekdays as befits her honor. The payment of the dowry shall be made at the time agreed upon [usually before the wedding ceremony].

    The wedding, for mazel tov, and in a propitious hour, shall take place at the time agreed upon. The bride's father will pay the emoluments for the officiating clergy [the rabbi, the cantor, and the sexton].

* Taken, with slight modifications, from Mendell Lewittes, *Jewish Marriage* (Northvale, NJ: Jason Aronson Inc., 1994).

All the above was accepted by both parties to confirm and establish a fine of half the value of the dowry to be paid by the party who cancels to the party who fulfills. The guarantors of this agreement: from the groom's part, Mr. N.; from the bride's part, Mr. N. The parties agree to reimburse the guarantors for any loss they may incur. And we made a kinyan with the parties on all that is stated and written above with a vessel fit for a kinyan, this being neither an asmakhta [presumptuous forfeiture].

And everything is firm and established.

Done in [city location] on the _____ day of the month of _____.

Testified by Witness _____

Testified by Witness _____

Parties _____

_____

The Reading of the Banns

The next step after getting engaged (solemnly or otherwise) was always the reading of the "banns," an old French word for "proclamation." Originally, this announcement formally publicized a couple's intention to marry so that if someone knew of a reason why the couple could not be lawfully married, he or she could bring this to the attention of the proper authorities before it was too late. But pragmatic considerations aside, reading the banns was a dramatic way of announcing the good news to a wider community and of building up suspense for the big day. They were always read from the pulpit on the three consecutive Sundays either following a solemn betrothal or prior to the wedding.

Roman Catholic

These simple banns were used — and in some places, are still used — by the Catholic Church in America.

> The banns of marriage are being read for the first [second or third] time for N. of [parish] and N. of [parish].

Lutheran

Martin Luther's 1529 marriage manual included this succinct suggestion on what to say when publishing the banns.

> N. and N. purpose to enter into the holy estate of matrimony according to God's ordinance. They desire that common Christian prayer be made on their behalf so that they may begin it in God's name and prosper therein. And should anyone have anything to say against it, let him speak in time or afterward hold his peace. God grant them His blessing. Amen.

Anglican/Episcopalian

This formula from the 1549 *Book of Common Prayer* became the staple not only for the Church of England but for the Episcopalian Church and many other American denominations (e.g., Methodist and Presbyterian) from the colonial period onwards.

> I publish the Banns of Marriage between N. of [parish] and N. of [parish]. If any of you know cause, or just impediment, why these two persons should not be joined in holy Matrimony, ye are to declare it. This is the first [second or third] time of asking.

Advice

BETROTHAL

We anticipate that your presider will be delighted with the idea of a solemn betrothal, since it is pastorally and theologically appealing, but it is a good idea to check with him as soon as possible, as there might be logistical obstacles. The church might be booked the day you want it or the minister unavailable to preside at that time. The sooner you iron out the time and setting, the better.

We should mention to Eastern Orthodox and Byzantine Catholic Christians that the betrothal rite we have included is generally done as the first part of the wedding ceremony. When this happens, it takes place in the vestibule of the church and is immediately followed by the Divine Liturgy (or Mass, to us Westerners) and the crowning, or rite of matrimony. The betrothal is placed so close to the wedding because a betrothal in Orthodox canon law came to be seen as binding as the marriage itself: it would even require an ecclesiastical divorce to dissolve. Consulting your Byzantine priest as to whether you can separate the betrothal from the marriage service would be a very good idea.

In-home betrothals are easier to do, but they still require an early coordination of everybody's schedule. Make sure to stress to all parties involved that this is not another wedding and will not require the same kind of preparation. It is not a bad idea, however, to have some "nuptial" elements present (like a boutonniere for the man and a nosegay for the woman) and perhaps even a short program.

One final suggestion: A betrothal ceremony could be coordinated with an engagement party which someone might be anxious to throw for you. Depending on the time of year, for example, one could have a short ceremony take place during a garden party.

READING THE BANNS

As we mentioned above, there is no longer a practical necessity for having the banns read. The practice, however, is still commendable, since it is a charming way of spreading the good news to your religious community. Again, we do not anticipate any objections from your pastor, though the customs of your parish must obviously take precedence.

Traditionally, as we mentioned above, the pastor reads the banns three Sundays in a row, either immediately after a solemn betrothal or (as is more common) immediately before the wedding. The usual time in the service is before the homily or whenever parish-related announcements are made. If your pastor agrees, give him or her a copy of the banns you have selected with your names already filled in.

Another idea is to have the banns published in your parish bulletin (a custom we have seen observed in some parishes). Find the person in charge of the bulletin and give him or her a copy identical to what you gave your pastor.

II. Feasts for the Ear, Feasts for the Eye: Music and Flowers

Then let the march tread our ears:
I to him turn with tears
Who to wedlock, his wonder wedlock,
Deals triumph and immortal years.

Gerard Manley Hopkins,
"At the Wedding March"

WHETHER IT IS THE MARCH, chanted psalms, service music, or special vocal solos, the music at one's wedding ceremony is of great importance. It is not the ceremony's essence, of course. Rather, it is its effervescence: A wedding without music is like a reception without champagne, and a wedding with so-so music is like a reception with bad champagne. In this chapter we will help you identify the sorts of music appropriate to the ceremony you are planning and the musical resources you have available to you. We will also make some specific recommendations of music pieces that are traditional without being clichés (see below) and which can be "auditioned" by consulting the list of albums we provide (see Appendix A). And we will give you some suggestions on how to find musicians capable of and interested in doing something special for your wedding.

A chapter focusing on nuptial effervescence, however, would not be complete without saying something about flowers. Like music, flowers are not essential to the wedding but have always been a beloved flourish. We will therefore conclude this chapter by acquainting you with the nuptial tradition of flowers and offering you concrete advice on how to make these traditions blossom at your own wedding.

Music

We divide the music into two categories: Marches and Service Music. However, there is no strict line between the two: A beautiful hymn may be appropriate as a recessional or processional or placed within the ceremony.

MARCHES

Originally the wedding service would have been held outside in the front porch of the church. Both newlyweds would then process inside for Mass, holding lit candles and chanting Psalm 128 (see below). When the service itself was moved to the church's interior, the procession became the bride's and the chant became a march.

Most people think of "Here Comes the Bride" from Wagner's *Lohengrin* or the wedding march from Mendelssohn's *A Midsummer Night's Dream* as the only orthodox options, but in fact the use of these marches is relatively new. (Also, because of Wagner's anti-Semitism and Mendelssohn's conversion to Christianity from Judaism, many rabbis will request that their music not be used at a Jewish wedding.) Princess Victoria, the eldest daughter of Queen Victoria, was a great fan of both composers, and chose both these marches for her 1858 wedding. Thus they became the royal standard, emulated both in Great Britain and the U.S. One interesting variation on this standard would be to have the Wagner march sung by a choir as it is in the opera — it is sung rather more softly than its organ transcription is usually played, and it would be a very nice, understated counterpoint to a more jubilant recessional march. But there are also many other appropriate and less-common pieces from which to choose.

In addition to the march (the **processional**), one should also have music when the guests are being seated (the **prelude**), music for the **mothers' entrance**, and music for the bride and groom's exit (the **recessional**). It is customary to choose a separate piece for each of these moments, and several pieces for the prelude. It is not appropriate, however, to have separate music for the bridesmaids and for the bride. In following royal custom, the bridesmaids are the heralds of the bride and thus do not have their own music to set them apart. The experienced organist and trumpeter will know exactly how to accentuate the piece to make certain everyone knows when the bride is ascending the aisle.

Prelude music (which has the benefit of quieting the guests before the ceremony) is generally played by an organist in a subdued tone. Any serene piece would be acceptable, though Bach's compositions tend to be the most popular choice. For the mothers' entrance we also suggest something serene, as you do not want it to dwarf the bridal march. The march itself should be jubilant in tone but not too fast for a bride and her father to follow. For the recessional, wherein the whole wedding party leaves together, we suggest something grand and stirring (like a good hymn), which organist, trumpeter, choir, and even the congregation can join, pulling out all the stops and raising the roof with a gladsome noise. As a general rule it is wise to have your musical selections ascend in grandeur and emotion, with the prelude as the most sedate and the recessional as the most exhilarating.

For musicians you will need to hire at least an organist and perhaps also a trumpeter. We also recommend a good choir or at least a good solo vocalist (see our advice on hiring at the end of this chapter). A sung march, for example, is both unusual and exceptionally joyous. Add an excellent trumpeter and your marches will be beyond beautiful — they will be glorious. A more exotic alternative — and one which we have seen used to great effect by Irish and Scottish families — is a bagpipe. The pipes can be used either instead of or in conjunction with the more conventional trumpet and organ. Their unmistakable timbre, combined with the custom of "piping the bride in" to the ceremony or reception by marching ahead of her in full clan garb — hat, jacket, and kilt — will add an unforgettable element to your nuptial festivities. We should add that there is no more plaintive and evocative instrument for outdoor processions (take care, though, that it doesn't overwhelm smaller venues).

The following list is obviously not exhaustive; you are sure to find many other beautiful and appropriate pieces from your own religious or ethnic traditions.

- The March from *Te Deum,* M.-A. Charpentier (Processional)
- "Diademata" ("Crown Him with Many Crowns"), George J. Elvey (Processional or Recessional)
- "Wachet Auf," J. S. Bach (Prelude or Mothers' Entrance)
- "Jesu, Joy of Man's Desiring," J. S. Bach (Mothers' Entrance or Processional)
- "Sheep May Safely Graze," J. S. Bach (Prelude or Mothers' Entrance)
- "Fanfare for Trumpet," J. J. Mouret (Processional or Recessional)
- "Trumpet Voluntary," Various (Purcell, Pachelbel, etc.) (Processional or Recessional)
- "Let the Bright Seraphim," *Samson,* G. F. Handel (Processional or Recessional)
- "Alleluia," J. S. Bach (Processional or Recessional)
- "Alle Psallite," twelfth century (Mothers' Entrance, Processional or Recessional)
- Various parts of Handel's *Water Music* and *Music for the Royal Fireworks*
- Hymns, Various (peruse the hymnals at your local church or synagogue for possible choices)

SERVICE MUSIC

By service music we mean music that is called for at particular times within the ceremony. If, for instance, your marriage is taking place within a Catholic nuptial Mass, you may choose to have many parts of the Mass sung, as well as having music sung at the offertory and communion. Many Catholic brides also like to include a Marian song, which is sung while the bride or couple bring flowers to Mary's altar (see Chapter VI).

At many Protestant weddings, Albert Hay Malotte's setting of the Lord's Prayer is favored. It remains that some priests and ministers prefer to have it recited as a common prayer.

While marches that begin and end the wedding ceremony are usually grand and ebullient, service music is softer, with emphasis on the meaning of the lyrics and often the corresponding liturgical action. This is the time to feature vocal soloists and choirs.

Psalms

A common feature of all weddings in the Jewish and Christian traditions is the use of psalms. It is not surprising that couples should turn to the psalms in their nuptial celebrations, since these inspired cries of joy and pain have always been cherished for their emotional candor and intimate familiarity with God. And the Psalter contains some of the most beautiful poetry in the world.

The following is a list of psalms traditionally used in marriage services. Each can be found in many different musical settings appropriate to different traditions: Hebrew, Latin, or English chant, polyphony and hymnody.

Psalm 45(44)*   "My heart hath uttered a good word . . ."
This psalm is traditionally chanted in Hebrew at a Jewish wedding while the bride and groom proceed from the entrance of the synagogue to the *chuppah*. With its erotic praise of the queen's beauty, the psalm is reminiscent of the nuptial imagery in the Song of Solomon. Note the verse, "The queen stood at Thy right hand, in gilded clothing." Both in position and in attire, this also describes the bride at a traditional Jewish wedding.

> My heart hath uttered a good word, I speak my works to the king;
> My tongue is the pen of a scrivener that writeth swiftly.

* Psalm numbers in the Hebrew Bible differ from those in the Greek Septuagint (which is given here and throughout in parentheses). Most Protestant churches follow the former while Catholic and Orthodox churches traditionally use the latter. As if this weren't confusing enough, the Catholic "New American" translation of the Bible follows the Hebrew reckoning.

Thou art beautiful above the sons of men;

Grace is poured abroad in thy lips; therefore hath God
blessed thee for ever.

Gird thy sword upon thy thigh, O thou most mighty.

With thy comeliness and thy beauty set out, proceed prosperously,
and reign,

Because of truth and meekness and justice; and thy right hand
shall conduct thee wonderfully.

Thy arrows are sharp; under thee shall people fall, into the hearts
of the king's enemies.

Thy throne, O God, is for ever and ever; the sceptre of thy kingdom
is a sceptre of righteousness.

Thou hast loved justice and hated iniquity; therefore God, thy God,
hath anointed thee with the oil of gladness above thy fellows.

Myrrh and stacte and cassia perfume thy garments,
from the ivory houses;

Out of which the daughters of kings have delighted thee
in thy glory.

The queen stood on thy right hand in gilded clothing;
surrounded with variety.

Hearken, O daughter, and see, and incline thy ear; and forget
thy people and thy father's house.

And the king shall greatly desire thy beauty; for he is the Lord
thy God, and him they shall adore.

And the daughters of Tyre with gifts, yea, all the rich among
the people, shall entreat thy countenance.

All the glory of the king's daughter is within golden borders,
clothed round about with varieties.

After her shall virgins be brought to the king; her neighbours
shall be brought to thee.

They shall be brought with gladness and rejoicing; they shall
be brought into the temple of the king.

Instead of thy fathers, sons are born to thee; thou shalt make them
princes over all the earth.

They shall remember thy name throughout all generations;

Therefore shall people praise thee for ever; yea, for ever and ever.

Psalm 67(66)   "May God have mercy on us, and bless us . . ."
This psalm was used in several medieval rites and was optional in the
Anglican service of Shakespeare's day. It is noteworthy for its beautiful
opening lines.

> May God have mercy on us, and bless us;
> May He cause the light of His countenance to shine upon us,
>   and may He have mercy on us.
> That we may know Thy way upon earth; Thy salvation
>   in all nations;
> Let people confess to Thee, O God; let all people give praise
>   to Thee.
> Let the nations be glad and rejoice; for Thou judgest the people
>   with justice, and directest the nations upon earth;
> Let the people, O God, confess to Thee; let all the people
>   give praise to Thee:
> The earth hath yielded her fruit; may God, our God, bless us.
> May God bless us; and all the ends of the earth fear Him.

Psalm 128(127)   "Blessed are all they that fear the Lord . . ."
If any of the psalms could be considered *the* Christian wedding psalm, it
is this one. Psalm 128 has been used at least since the 300s for weddings
and appears — among other places — in the Anglican service of Shakespeare's day, in the Catholic nuptial Mass from late Roman times until
the 1960s, in Luther's marriage hymn "Happy Who in God's Fear Doth
Stay," in John Knox's 1556 "Forme of Marriage" for the (Presbyterian)
Church of Scotland, and in the Byzantine liturgies of the East, ancient
and contemporary. (In addition to Luther's hymn, it can also be found in
Gregorian chant in Latin or in a number of Eastern chant settings in various languages.) Instead of the queen's beauty, this psalm describes a
God-fearing man blessed by a large family and ends with a sentiment
prominent in many Christian marriage prayers: "Mayest thou see thy
children's children."

> Blessed are all they that fear the Lord, that walk in His ways.
> For thou shalt eat the labours of thy hands; blessed art thou,
>   and it shall be well with thee;

Thy wife as a fruitful vine, on the sides of thy house;
Thy children as olive plants, round about thy table.
Behold, thus shall the man be blessed that feareth the Lord.
May the Lord bless thee out of Sion; and mayest thou see
        the good things of Jerusalem all the days of thy life.
And mayest thou see thy children's children: peace upon Israel.

Masses

If you will be married at a Catholic or Anglican Mass, you can choose a sung Mass by some of the world's greatest composers of sacred music — provided, of course, that you can find someone willing and able to perform it (on this, please see the last section of this chapter). Most Masses by great composers were written in Latin, but there are some beautiful Masses in English, both polyphonic and chanted, by contemporary composers — one just has to look a little harder for them. There is, however, no obstacle to having Latin sung even at an English Mass — some of your older guests will love hearing it again.

Here is a list of a few Masses appropriate to the spirit of a nuptial Mass:

- *Missa de Angelis, Gregorian Mass IX* — or almost any chant Mass, though one should avoid the most familiar — the Mass for the dead!
- *Missa Brevis,* Palestrina — this exquisite polyphonic composition can be successfully sung with only four or five voices
- *Missa Secunda,* Hans Leo Hassler — like the Palestrina, this Mass can be performed by a choir of at least four voices of considerable skill, but both are reasonably easy for professional musicians to learn
- *Mass in G Major,* Franz Schubert — If your budget allows for a full choir and string quartet, why not give your wedding the royal treatment?
- *Missa Brevis,* by the contemporary composer Sean McDermott

Other Music

There are many other opportunities for music at weddings. These are some of our favorites, which you may find appropriate at various points in your wedding ceremony.

- "If Ye Love Me," Thomas Tallis
- "May God Smile on You," J. S. Bach — a beautiful duet appropriate for Jewish and Christian weddings
- "Whither Thou Goest," Flor Peeters
- "Come My Way, My Truth, My Life," Ralph Vaughan Williams
- "Panis Angelicus," C. Franck
- "Ave Maria," set by Gounod, Victoria, or Schubert — or other less common Marian songs, e.g., "Dixit Maria," Hans Leo Hassler; "Alma Redemptoris Mater," Palestrina; "Hail Holy Queen Enthroned Above," etc.
- "The Lord's Prayer," Albert Hay Malotte
- "This Is the Day," by the contemporary composer Stephen Grimm

Wedding Score Samples

In Appendix A you will find a relatively comprehensive list of wedding albums. These compilations — to say nothing of what can be down-loaded from the internet — will make it easy for you to hear all of the classical works generally associated with weddings. But hearing is one thing, deciding another. Since having a vast range of options can make choosing more difficult, we include here a sample of wedding music programs divided according to the kind of musical instrument and num-ber of voices used. This will allow you to see not only how various pieces fit together, but what pieces are most adaptable to the re-sources at your disposal. As you read these programs, keep in mind that music can be transcribed and arranged for numerous combinations of instruments, and each combination will have its own particular ef-fect. A good musician will thus be able to adapt pieces to your choice of instrument(s); and this is a service that may be well worth factoring into your musical budget if you have favorite selections that are usually performed in different settings.

For Organ

A solo organist is an ideal arrangement for the financially strained wedding planner or the lover of simplicity. (Pianos, while also fitting these criteria, should be avoided in congregational settings — they produce too intimate a sound for typical church acoustics.)

Sample A

Prelude:	"Sheep May Safely Graze," J. S. Bach
Mothers' Entrance:	"Air," *Water Music*, G. F. Handel
Processional:	"Toccata," *5th Symphony for Organ*, C.-M. Widor
Recessional:	"Praise We Sing to Thee," F. J. Haydn

Sample B

Prelude:	Sinfonia in F, J. S. Bach
Mothers' Entrance:	"Blest Be the Tie That Binds," Hans Nageli
Processional:	Voluntary in D, Maurice Greene
Recessional:	"Diademata" ("Crown Him with Many Crowns"), G. Elvey

Sample C

Prelude:	"Jesu, Joy of Man's Desiring," J. S. Bach
Mothers' Entrance:	Canon in D, Pachelbel
Processional:	March from *Te Deum*, M.-A. Charpentier
Recessional:	Prelude & Fugue in D, J. S. Bach

For Organ and Trumpet

The most popular arrangement today is having one organist and one trumpeter. These pieces were chosen with both in mind.

Sample A

Prelude:	"Suite Gaillarde," M. Praetorius
Mothers' Entrance:	"Bourée," *Water Music*, G. F. Handel

| Processional: | "Fanfare for Trumpet," J. J. Mouret |
| Recessional: | "Prince of Denmark's March," J. Clarke |

Sample B

Prelude:	"Meditation," *Thaïs*, Massenet
Mothers' Entrance:	"Wachet Auf," J. S. Bach
Processional:	"The Highland Wedding," A. MacKay
Recessional:	Trumpet Voluntary, A. Stradella

Sample C

Prelude:	"Festal Fanfare," anon.
Mothers' Entrance:	"Hornpipe," *Water Music*, G. F. Handel
Processional:	March from *Te Deum*, M.-A. Charpentier
Recessional:	Trumpet Voluntary, J. Stanley

For String Quartet

A string quartet would make an elegant addition to any organ and trumpet ensemble.

Sample A: For Quartet

Prelude:	Canon in D, Pachelbel
Mothers' Entrance:	"Largo," *Xerxes*, G. F. Handel
Processional:	"Bridal March," *Lohengrin*, R. Wagner
Recessional:	"The Married Beau," H. Purcell

Sample B: For Organ and Quartet

Prelude:	"Bonduca," H. Purcell
Mothers' Entrance:	"Sposalizio," A. Gabrieli
Processional:	"Amphitryon," H. Purcell
Recessional:	"Arrival of the Queen of Sheba,"
	Solomon, G. F. Handel

Sample C: For Organ, Trumpet, and Quartet

Prelude:	"Alleluia," J. S. Bach
Mothers' Entrance:	"The Old Bachelor," H. Purcell
Processional:	"The Indian Queen," H. Purcell

| Recessional: | "March," *A Midsummer Night's Dream*, F. Mendelssohn |

For Choir

A choir is a glorious enrichment of any musical feast, and is especially welcome at weddings that involve more than simply the nuptial service (for example, a wedding that includes a Mass). As we stated at the beginning of the chapter, choirs can be used in processionals as well, but they are perhaps more appropriately placed at the end for a stirring recessional.

Sample A: For Organ and Choir
Prelude:	"May God Smile on You," J. S. Bach
Mothers' Entrance:	"Prayer of St. Gregory," A. Hovhaness
Processional:	"The Coolin," S. Barber
Service	*Missa de Angelis, Gregorian Mass IX*
Recessional:	"Alle Psallite," anon.

Sample B: For Organ, Trumpet, and Choir
Prelude:	"If Ye Love Me," T. Tallis
Mothers' Entrance:	"Now Let All the Heavens Adore Thee," J. S. Bach
Processional:	"Prince of Denmark's March," J. Clarke
Service:	*Missa Brevis*, Palestrina
Recessional:	"This Is the Day," Stephen Grimm

Sample C: For Organ, Trumpet, Quartet, and Choir
Prelude:	"Exsultate, Jubilate," W. A. Mozart
Mothers' Entrance:	"Bis du bei mir" ("If Thou Be Near"), J. S. Bach
Processional:	March from *Te Deum*, M.-A. Charpentier
Service:	*Mass in G Major*, F. Schubert
Recessional:	"Let the Bright Seraphim," *Samson*, G. F. Handel

Flowers

If flowers are, as the poet says, love's truest language, then their enduring popularity at weddings is of little wonder. The use of flowers in nuptial celebrations goes back at least as far as the pagan decoration of the marriage-bed in ancient Greece, but the custom took root (no pun intended) within the marriage service as well. In biblical times a Jewish bride wore a gold crown if her family were wealthy or a crown of orange blossoms if they were not (though after the destruction of the Holy Temple in A.D. 70 the gold crown was forbidden as a token of sorrow). In fact, because of their association with chastity, orange blossoms have come to be the traditional flower of choice among Western brides — Jewish, Christian, and even Muslim. (Of course, there is an exception to every rule: The Austrian bride traditionally prefers myrtle, the "flower of life.") Flowers eventually found their way onto the rest of the wedding party as well. In France, for example, it was customary for the bride to give her maids white flowers while the groom gave his men red.

Decorating the sanctuary with flowers is also a time-honored practice. Again in France, "flower-banks" would cover the *prie-dieu* on which a couple knelt during the service, while altar flowers were welcome in even the most Puritan churches of nineteenth-century England and America. This was especially true in Victorian times, when elaborate lexicons detailing the meaning of different flowers were widely circulated. Flowers could even take on a liturgical significance: Each saint in the church calendar once had his own flower. But more often than not flowers simply ended up being the favored choice of this or that culture. The Welsh, for example, use myrtle at their weddings, while the Czechs prefer rosemary. And sometimes a plant does not even have to be a flower in order for it to be a favorite, as the Scandinavian wedding custom of adorning their churches with birch branches bears out.

While the tradition of using flowers in the wedding is well established, the rules regarding exactly what flowers to use are not. We have compiled a list of flowers potentially useful in a bridal bouquet or in the sanctuary and have culled their meaning from several Victorian tomes (this list can be found in Appendix B). Be advised, however, that our list is neither exhaustive nor definitive. Moreover, other factors — such as the color of your wedding, the season of the year, and the general rules of aesthetics — should take precedence. Our practical advice on the subject is given, as always, at the end of the chapter.

Advice

MUSIC

It is one thing to know that you want music that is at once unusual, traditional, and beautiful at your wedding. It is altogether a different matter knowing how to find musicians able to perform such music. If you approach good musicians with a clear idea of what you prefer, however — for example, chant, Renaissance polyphony, Baroque, or Romantic — you should do fine.

The first place to begin, both for practical and protocol reasons, is with the music director of the church where you will be married. In many parishes, the organist must be consulted and sometimes even paid a "bench fee" if you hire someone else to play for your wedding. Thus, it may be sensible to consider the church organist first for the job. Even if the music you hear in Sunday services would lead you to look elsewhere, you may find that your local music director is able and even eager to do something excellent for your wedding. Music directors don't often have sole control over their choices for regular services and may be excited by the chance to do more diverse music. Likewise, if your church has a good choir, consider hiring it or perhaps a few members of it for a smaller ensemble. On the other hand, be forewarned that church musicians often have a set repertoire for weddings, and may be unwilling to learn pieces unfamiliar to them.

What to do if your church has no musicians or none that are capable of the music you want? Its music director may be able to direct you to first-class musicians. Local symphony orchestras, community choruses, or master chorales are good starting points. Music schools and music departments of colleges and universities are additional sources of both instrumentalists and vocalists. If you want a small choir, you might even post a notice on a music school bulletin board looking for students who would be willing to form an *ad hoc* choir (both for the experience and the money). Other local churches may also be good places to look and listen. Be sure, however, to audition or listen to the demo tapes of any musicians you haven't heard performing the sort of music you want — better to have modest music done well than ambitious music done poorly. One note, however, that we have heard church musicians repeatedly sound: Secular love songs should be saved for the reception, as they are never appropriate for the service. The music director of your church can provide specifics on what is appropriate sacred music within your denomination. It is also important to remember that if you want special music at your wedding, you must give your musicians plenty of time to locate and rehearse it.

This brings us to one final piece of advice. You should choose your musicians according to the sort of music you want at your ceremony. However, once you have found your musicians, work with them to decide what specific music will be played at the ceremony. They may already know pieces that will fit your ceremony which you haven't heard. But do find people who are willing to work with your desires, and are open to learning new music if need be. Once you have gauged their good faith, however, give them space to do their jobs. They will be as concerned as you to make your ceremony one of beauty and excellence.

FLOWERS

Planning the flowers for your wedding can be made considerably easier by a timely beginning. Keeping in mind that you will probably have to meet with a few different florists before you find the right fit, you should start making appointments as early as possible. (Though some florists may not want to meet with you until a few months before the wedding, they can be persuaded by your persistence.) Always begin your search with the best florist in town. Even if it is likely that his or her fees will be prohibitive, the experience will give you a number of ideas instrumental in shaping your own vision. Remember, however, that vision alone cannot turn a bad florist into a good one. Make certain that you first see samples of his or her work. The cost of the finest florist might be worth the sacrifice after all.

Before meeting with the florist, do your homework. Peruse floral books, magazines (the bridal and garden kinds are usually the best), and even your friends' wedding photos for ideas. Cut out magazine pictures of your favorite bouquets and arrangements, and discuss their feasibility when you meet with your florist. Do not, however, make yourself both customer and designer. Try to strike the right balance between knowing what you want and listening to the wisdom of the professional.

Given the expenses that a wedding can incur, many couples decide against spending a great deal on flowers. This can be done without aesthetic sacrifice by focusing your attention on a few key places. You may be tempted to forgo flowers at the ceremony, but considering that the church is the first place your guests will be (as well as the fact that they might be there for a good amount of time), a few tasteful arrangements will be well worth the money. There are usually only two areas that need flowers: the door or entrance to the church and the sanctuary. A swag or half basket of flowers on the door of the church is a delightful way to greet guests and to set the tone for the ceremony. This usually consists of cut flowers, but one can also opt for seasonal potted plants. Potted plants are not only less expensive, but they can later be planted in the yard to serve as a lovely reminder of your wedding day (this is especially true if the plants are perennials). Finally, ribbons and bows on the door are a low-cost alternative to flowers and have the advantage of being able to be coordinated with the aisle decoration inside.

One large arrangement placed atop a pedestal is all that is really necessary for altar flowers. (Normally it is preferable to have one large arrangement rather than two smaller ones.) The flowers for this arrangement do not have to be the best and most expensive — their visibility from the pews is more important — but they should be cut. Traditionally, only those objects which have been separated, or "cut off," from everyday use are allowed in the sanctuary of a church. Respecting this custom, however, does not prevent you from taking the arrangements from the church to the reception, another time-honored, cost-saving measure. If you decide to do this, remember that baskets are easier to transport than vases, and make certain that the person transporting the arrangements knows exactly what to do with them.

Churches sometimes book more than one wedding for a single day or weekend. If this is the case, you may be able to contact the other bridal party and see if they would like to share arrangements with you. If, on the other hand, you are getting married near a holiday such as

Christmas or Easter, the church might already have elaborate decorations in place.

When it comes to incorporating the meanings of flowers into your bouquets, keep in mind that less is more. Trying to make every flower symbolize something will tax the sanity of both you and your florist. Perhaps having one symbolic flower in the bride's bouquet or groom's boutonniere is sufficient. Orange blossom or lily of the valley for the bridal bouquet, for example, is a wonderful token of the bride's purity, while the groom's boutonniere can be meaningfully enriched with ivy (fidelity) or a daisy (innocence). Again your florist will be instrumental in helping you strike the right balance.

III. Holy Writ: Allocutions and Readings

For we, which now
behold these present days,
Have eyes to wonder,
but lack tongues to praise.

Shakespeare,
Sonnet CVI

A TRADITIONAL WEDDING is not only a time of celebration but a time of reflection. Biblical passages on marriage as well as a pastor's opening addresses to the couple (called an "allocution") have always served to enlighten and inform the warm sentiments which everyone feels on this special day. This chapter will present a variety of famous allocutions throughout the ages and will list Scripture's "well-worn" nuptial passages, citing not only chapter and verse, but where and when they were popular. Finally, we will offer some suggestions on how to make the right biblical and homiletical choices for your wedding.

Allocutions

The nuptial allocution has always been a part of the marriage service, as pastors have always been careful to educate the couple about their new life and eager to encourage them to get the most out of it. The allocution can appear either as an opening address or as the sermon that follows the scriptural readings.

Eighteenth-Century America

We are tempted to call this classic and well-known opening from the 1790 Episcopalian service the "American" allocution, not only because it was later adopted by many American denominations, but because it reflects the unadorned elegance of the Yankee spirit.

> Dearly beloved, we are gathered together here in the sight of God and in the face of this company, to join together this Man and this Woman in holy Matrimony, which is commended of St. Paul to be honourable among all men; and therefore it is not to be entered into unadvisedly or lightly; but reverently, discreetly, advisedly, soberly, and in the fear of God. Into this holy estate these two persons present now come to be joined. Therefore, if any man can show just cause, why they may not lawfully be joined together, let him now speak, or else hereafter for ever hold his peace.

Elizabethan England

The "American" allocution is an abridgment of its older and more elaborate English cousin, used in Shakespeare's day.

> Dearly beloved friends, we are gathered together here in the sight of God, and in the face of his congregation, to join together this man and this woman in holy Matrimony; which is an honourable estate, instituted of God in Paradise, in the time of man's innocency, signifying unto us the mystical union that is betwixt Christ and his

Church: which holy estate, Christ adorned and beautified with his presence and first miracle that he wrought in Cana of Galilee, and is commended of Saint Paul, to be honourable among all men, and therefore is not to be enterprised, or taken in hand unadvisedly, lightly, or wantonly, to satisfy men's carnal lusts and appetites, like brute beasts that have no understanding: but reverently, discreetly, advisedly, soberly, and in the fear of God, duly considering the causes for the which matrimony was ordained.

One was, the procreation of children, to be brought up in the fear and nurture of the Lord, and praise of God. Secondly, it was ordained for a remedy against sin, and to avoid fornication, that such persons as have not the gift of continency might marry, and keep themselves undefiled members of Christ's body. Thirdly, for the mutual society, help, and comfort, that the one ought to have of the other, both in prosperity and adversity: into the which holy estate, these two persons present come now to be joined. Therefore if any man can shew any just cause, why they may not lawfully be joined together, let him now speak, or hereafter for ever hold his peace.

LUTHER'S GERMANY

From Paul to Solomon: Martin Luther's sermon artfully combines curse, comfort, and political incorrectness.

Since both of you have entered the married estate in God's name, hear first of all God's commandment concerning this estate. Thus speaketh Saint Paul: "Husbands, love your wives, even as Christ also loved the church, and gave himself for it; that he might sanctify and cleanse it with the washing of water by the word, that he might present it to himself a glorious church, not having spot or blemish. So ought men to love their wives as their own bodies. He that loveth his wife loveth himself. For no man ever yet hated his own flesh; but nourisheth and cherisheth it, even as the Lord the church. Wives, submit yourselves unto your husbands, as unto the Lord. For the husband is the head of the wife, even as Christ is the head of the church: and he is the savior of the body. Therefore as the church is subject unto Christ, so let wives be to their own husbands in every thing."

Second, hear also the cross which God has placed upon this estate. God spake thus to the woman: "I will greatly multiply thy sorrow and thy conception; in sorrow thou shalt bring forth children; and thy desire shall be to thy husband, and he shall rule over thee." And God spake thus to the man: "Because thou hast hearkened unto the voice of thy wife, and hast eaten of the tree, of which I commanded thee, saying, 'Thou shalt not eat of It,' cursed is the ground for thy sake; in sorrow shalt thou eat of it all the days of thy life; thorns and thistles shall it bring forth to thee; and thou shalt eat the herb of the field; in the sweat of thy face shalt thou eat bread, till thou return unto the ground; for out of it wast thou taken: for dust thou art, and unto dust shalt thou return."

Third, this is your comfort that you may know and believe that your estate is pleasing to God and blessed by him. For it is written: "God created man in his own image, in the image of God he created him; male and female he created them. And God blessed them, and said unto them, 'Be fruitful and multiply, and replenish the earth, and subdue it: and have dominion over the fish of the sea, and over the fowl of the air, and over every living thing that moveth upon the earth.' And God saw every thing that he had made, and behold, it was very good." Therefore, Solomon also says: "Who so findeth a wife findeth a good thing, and obtaineth favor of the Lord."

CALVIN'S GENEVA

Calvin was not a man known to mince words, as this stern yet erudite opening address from his 1542 Marriage Service illustrates:

God our Father, after having created heaven and earth and all that is in them, created and formed man in His image and likeness, man who has dominion and lordship over the beasts of the earth, the fish of the sea, the birds of the sky. And after having created man God said: "It is not good for man to be alone; let Us make for him a help like unto himself." And our Lord cast a deep sleep upon Adam; and as Adam slept God took one of his ribs and formed Eve, thus giving to understand that man and woman are but one body, one flesh, and one blood. This is why a man leaves father and mother and cleaves to his wife, whom he should love as Jesus loves His Church — that is to say, the truly faithful Christians for whom He died.

And so a woman should serve and obey her husband in all sanctity and honesty because she is subject to and under the power of the husband as long as she lives with him. And this holy and honorable Matrimony, instituted by God, is of such virtue that the husband no longer has power over his own body; the woman does. And the woman no longer has power over her body; the man does. This is why, having been joined by God, they cannot be separated, except at some times by the consent of both in order to fast, being on guard all the while to pray that Satan might not tempt them with incontinence. Nevertheless, they should return to each other. For, in order to avoid fornication, each man should have his wife, and each wife her husband in such a manner that all those who cannot be continent and who do not have the gift of continence are obligated, by the commandment of God, to marry: so that the holy temple of God (that is to say, our bodies) not be violated and corrupted. For because our bodies are members of Jesus Christ, it would be a great outrage to make them members of lewdness. This is why one should keep them in all sanctity. For if anyone violates the temple of God, God will destroy him.

NINETEENTH-CENTURY FRANCE

Allocutions were a part of Catholic weddings too. Here is an example from an 1839 Paris manual which, in a style peppered with French warmth, describes the great dignity and obligations of Christian marriage:

My dear brother and my dear sister,

God Himself, from the beginning of the world, instituted marriage to unite a couple by a bond as sacred as it is unbreakable. Since men, having corrupted their ways, eventually forgot the excellence of this union; since it was dishonored by the divorces of pagans; since, among the Hebrews of old, it was not maintained in all its perfection, Jesus Christ re-established it to its original state; and not only did He declare this alliance one and indissoluble — as it was from its very institution — but He even elevated it to the dignity of a sacrament. The marriage of Christians is therefore a sacred fellowship that the Savior of mankind has consecrated by His grace and that the Apostle calls a "great sacrament" — great because of the mystery of which it is a symbol (representing the union of Jesus Christ with His Church); great, by the precious graces of which it is the source; great, by the sacred obligations that it imposes. Such are, my dear brother and my dear sister, the truths which should at this time be occupying your spirit, animating your faith, exciting your devotion. These are the principal obligations which this sacrament will impose on you and which demand on your part the most serious reflection.

"We are the children of saints," once said the young Tobias to his wife. "We ought not to live in marriage as the nations who do not know the Lord." This ought to be, with even more justice, the words of Christian spouses. Holy by their status as children of God (which they have received from their baptism), they ought not to engage in marriage except with holy views. They ought to live in holiness, according to the Lord, and not following the maxims of a perverse world. They ought to render their union honorable by the purity of their actions and by a mutual and inviolable fidelity. Finally, if it pleases Heaven to bless their alliance with fruitfulness, they ought to give their children a Christian education and to form them in virtue, more by their examples than by their instructions.

You have these obligations in common, my dear brother and my dear sister: now learn of your particular duties. Husband, love your wife as Jesus Christ loved His Church, cherishing her as a part of yourself. Heaven has given you dominion over her; but so that a tender love may always guide the use of your authority, heed the words of Saint Ambrose — "It is not a slave, it is a wife, you have gained" — that your care, your attention, and your respect may make her forget or even love her dependence. And you, wife, be subject to your husband, as the Church is subject to Jesus Christ. "The husband," says the Apostle, "is the head of his wife, as Jesus Christ is the head of the Church." May your sweetness ward off all which could disrupt the peace which should reign between you; may your modesty, a lovable reserve, constantly speak to him of your heart and of your fidelity. Remember that virtue is infinitely more precious than all external advantages. "The woman who fears the Lord," says the Sage, "alone merits praise. She will be the joy of her husband, and she will make him to dwell in peace all the days of his life."

In fulfilling all these obligations faithfully, Christian spouses, the blessings of Heaven will descend upon you and your posterity. And you will find that your union will not only be a source of happiness in this world, but that it will also be for you a powerful means of salvation.

Bible Readings

The Bible has much to say about the joy and meaning of marriage, making it the perfect voice for a couple about to embark on their new journey. Not surprisingly, selections from the Scriptures are an intrinsic part of most Christian and Jewish services.

For the sake of brevity we are limiting ourselves to only those passages traditionally used in Judeo-Christian weddings. Special mention, however, should be made here of two other selections. First, ever since the 1969 New Catholic Rite of Matrimony made optional a "First Reading" from the Old Testament in addition to a "Second Reading" (Epistle) from the New, many Roman Catholics have chosen Tobias (Tobit) 7:6-14, the beautiful love story of Tobias and Sara, for their first reading. Equally notable as a second reading is I Corinthians 13, the famous "love is patient, love is kind" passage from St. Paul. Though it does not describe conjugal love per se but the divinely bestowed gift of *agape,* or charity (and for this reason it is not found in traditional services), this selection has become popular at weddings in the last thirty years or so.

THE "EPISTLE"

Christian Liturgies of the Word traditionally contain two readings from Scripture. The first usually consists of a passage from one of the New Testament epistles (though passages from the Old Testament were also used), while the second is a passage taken from one of the four Gospels. We are working within the framework of this custom, though it is now possible in most Christian marriage services today to have three separate readings — the first from the Old Testament, the second from a New Testament Epistle, and the third from a Gospel.

I Corinthians 6:15-20

Popular in Europe from the sixth century on in Rome, France, and England, this passage strongly encourages a chaste and faithful marriage:

> Know you not that your bodies are the members of Christ? Shall I then take the members of Christ, and make them the members of an harlot? God forbid. Or know you not, that he who is joined to a harlot, is made one body? For they shall be, saith He, two in one flesh. But he who is joined to the Lord, is one spirit.
>
> Flee fornication. Every sin that a man doth is without the body; but he that committeth fornication, sinneth against his own body. Or know you not, that your members are the temple of the Holy Spirit, who is in you, whom you have from God, and that you are not your own? For you are bought with a great price. Glorify and bear God in your body.

Isaiah 61:10, 11

This beautiful description of deliverance as a couple on their wedding day was used in ninth-century France:

> I will greatly rejoice in the Lord, and my soul shall be joyful in my God, for He hath clothed me with the garments of salvation: and with the robe of justice He hath covered me, as a bridegroom decked with a crown, and as a bride adorned with her jewels.
>
> For as the earth bringeth forth her bud, and as the garden causeth her seed to shoot forth: so shall the Lord God make justice to spring forth, and praise before all the nations.

Ephesians 5:22-33

At first blush Paul's admonition to husbands and wives sounds like a rationale for male chauvinism, until one realizes that he is telling a man to rule by *serving,* including sacrificing his very life. Not only does this empty the husband's headship of all machismo and place on him a humbling obligation, but it underscores the dignity of a Christian married woman. This passage was used in the Anglican Church's sermon, by the Roman Catholic Church from the 1500s (and sometimes earlier) until the 1960s, and by the Byzantine Catholic and Orthodox churches from the early Middle Ages up to the present day.

> Let women be subject to their husbands, as to the Lord. Because the husband is the head of the wife, as Christ is the head of the Church. He is the saviour of His body. Therefore as the Church is subject to Christ, so also let the wives be to their husbands in all things. Husbands, love your wives, as Christ also loved the Church, and delivered Himself up for it, that He might sanctify it, cleansing it by the laver of water in the word of life: that He might present it to Himself a glorious Church, not having spot or wrinkle, or any such thing; but that it should be holy and without blemish. So also ought men to love their wives as their own bodies. He that loveth his wife, loveth himself. For no man ever hated his own flesh; but nourisheth and cherisheth it, as also Christ doth the Church, be-

cause we are members of his body, of his flesh, and of his bones. For this cause shall a man leave his father and mother, and shall cleave to his wife, and they shall be two in one flesh. This is a great sacrament; but I speak in Christ and in the Church. Nevertheless, let every one of you in particular love his wife as himself, and let the wife fear her husband.*

Genesis 2:18, 21-24

Aptly enough, Luther's Marriage Service contained the biblical account of the first marriage by the first Matchmaker. Adam's experience of waking from a deep sleep to find himself in love is one to which many men on their way to the altar can relate.

> And the Lord God said, "It is not good for man to be alone: let Us make him a help like unto himself." Then the Lord God cast a deep sleep upon Adam: and when he was fast asleep, He took one of his ribs, and filled up flesh for it. And the Lord God built the rib which He took from Adam into a woman: and brought her to Adam. And Adam said: "This now is bone of my bones, and flesh of my flesh; she shall be called woman, because she was taken out of man." Wherefore a man shall leave father and mother and shall cleave to his wife: and they shall be two in one flesh.

Hosea 2:16, 18-20, 24

This arresting pledge by YHWH to wed His beloved Israel makes an ideal selection for a Jewish wedding. In sharp contrast to the picture of infidelity painted in the verses preceding this passage, the prophet Hosea now describes the power of that perfect and peaceful espousal upon which Jewish and Christian marriages are based:

> "And it shall be in that day," saith the Lord, "that she shall call me, 'My husband,' and she shall call me Baal no more.

* Some modern translations use "be in awe of" instead of "fear" in order to translate the Greek verb used here.

"And in that day I will make a covenant with them, with the beasts of the field, and with the fowls of the air, and with the creeping things of the earth; and I will destroy the bow, and the sword, and war out of the land; and I will make them sleep secure.

"And I will espouse thee to Me for ever; and I will espouse thee to Me in justice, and judgment, and in mercy, and in commiserations.

"And I will espouse thee to Me in faith; and thou shalt know that I am the Lord.

"And I will say to that which was not my people: 'Thou art my people'; and they shall say: 'Thou art my God.'"

THE GOSPEL

Matthew 19:3-6

Jesus brings to its logical conclusion the Genesis statement about two becoming one flesh by declaring marriage indissoluble. This passage was widely used in the Middle Ages in France, England, Ireland, and Germany, and was universally used both by Roman Catholics from the 1500s to the 1960s and by Calvin's early followers. In fact, John Knox's "Forme of Marriage" for the Church of Scotland instructs the pastor to tell the couple that this Gospel is being read "that ye may understande . . . howe sure and faste a knott marriage is"!

And there came to Him the Pharisees tempting Him and saying: "Is it lawful for a man to put away his wife for every cause?" Who answering, said to them: "Have ye not read, that He who made man from beginning, 'made them male and female'? And He said: 'For this cause shall a man leave father and mother, and shall cleave to his wife, and they two shall be in one flesh.' Therefore now they are not two, but one flesh. What therefore God hath joined together, let no man put asunder."

John 2:1-11

The account of Christ's first public miracle was seen as not only captur-
ing the joy of the wedding feast, but as a sign of what Christ, through
His mother's intercession, brings to a marriage. It was used in parts of
England at least as far back as the 800s, and in the Byzantine liturgies of
yesterday and today:

> And on the third day, there was a marriage in Cana of Galilee: and
> the mother of Jesus was there. And Jesus also was invited, and His
> disciples, to the marriage. And the wine failing, the mother of Jesus
> saith to Him: "They have no wine." And Jesus saith to her: "Woman,
> what is that to Me and to thee? My hour is not yet come." His
> mother saith to the waiters: "Whatsoever He shall say to you, do
> ye."
>
> Now there were set there six waterpots of stone, according to
> the manner of the purifying of the Jews, containing two or three
> measures apiece. Jesus saith to them: "Fill the waterpots with wa-
> ter." And they filled them up to the brim. And Jesus saith to them:
> "Draw out now, and carry to the chief steward of the feast." And
> they carried it. And when the wine steward had tasted the water
> made wine, and knew not whence it was (but the waiters knew who
> had drawn the water), the chief steward calleth the bridegroom and
> saith to him: "Every man at first setteth forth good wine, and when
> men have well drunk, then that which is worse. But thou hast kept
> the good wine until now."
>
> This beginning of miracles did Jesus in Cana of Galilee; and
> manifested His glory, and His disciples believed in Him.

Matthew 22:2-14

This parable compares the Kingdom of God to a marriage feast. It was
used in the 800s in Durham, England.

> The kingdom of heaven is likened to a king who made a marriage
> for his son. And he sent his servants to call them that were invited
> to the marriage; and they would not come. Again he sent other ser-

vants, saying: "Tell them that were invited, 'Behold, I have prepared my dinner; my oxen and fatlings are killed, and all things are ready: come ye to the marriage.'" But they neglected, and went their ways, one to his farm, and another to his merchandise. And the rest laid hands on his servants, and having treated them contumaciously, put them to death. But when the king had heard of it, he was angry, and sending his armies, he destroyed those murderers and burnt their city.

Then he saith to his servants: "The marriage indeed is ready; but they that were invited were not worthy. Go ye therefore into the highways; and as many as you shall find, call to the marriage." And his servants going forth into the ways, gathered together all that they found, both bad and good; and the marriage was filled with guests.

And the king went in to see the guests. And he saw there a man who had not on a wedding garment. And he saith to him: "Friend, how camest thou in hither not having on a wedding garment?" But he was silent. Then the king said to the waiters: "Bind his hands and feet, and cast him into the exterior darkness; there shall be weeping and gnashing of teeth." For many are called, but few are chosen.

John 3:27-29

John the Baptist is asked by his disciples about the growing prominence of Jesus of Nazareth. John's response, recorded here by the Apostle John, became the Gospel of choice in several nuptial rites of the early Middle Ages.

John answered and said: "A man cannot receive any thing, unless it be given him from heaven. You yourselves do bear witness that I said, 'I am not Christ, but that I am sent from Him.' He that hath the bride is the bridegroom, but the friend of the bridegroom, who standeth and heareth him, rejoiceth with joy because of the bridegroom's voice. This, my joy, therefore is fulfilled."

Between the two different ceremonies which comprise a Jewish wedding lies a sort of liturgical intermission. This space, which follows the public reading of the marriage contract, or *ketubah* (see Chapter V), is generally filled by a short sermon from the rabbi and a reading from the Scriptures. Traditionally, this reading is taken from the Bible's most erotic book — the Song of Solomon. We include one passage (2:10-14,16) especially appropriate for a spring or summer wedding, though not with the intention of precluding other equally suitable selections.

> Behold my beloved speaketh to me: "Arise, make haste, my love, my dove, my beautiful one, and come. For winter is past, the rain is over and gone. The flowers have appeared in our land, the time of pruning is come; the voice of the turtle is heard in our land. The fig tree hath put forth her green figs; the vines in flower yield their sweet smell. Arise, my love, my beautiful one, and come. My dove in the clefts of the rock, in the hollow places of the wall, shew me thy face, let thy voice sound in my ears. For thy voice is sweet, and thy face comely. . . ." My beloved is mine and I am his who feedeth among the lilies.

Advice

READINGS

Most churches and synagogues today allow a fair amount of flexibility in choosing scriptural readings for your wedding (see Appendix C for the current Roman Catholic options). In making selections, try to choose ones that go together well. Perhaps they may say the same thing but in different ways, or they may present complementary sides of the same coin; either way, they should somehow form one harmonious teaching. This should not be too difficult given the fact that the Bible is ultimately consistent in its teaching, but this rule of thumb should nevertheless be kept in mind. Also, try to select a passage that somehow bears on your lives as husband and wife. The passage could do this by speaking poignantly to your heart, or it may simply be that it was used at a time or place to which you can relate. It would certainly not be inappropriate to choose a passage on the grounds that it was used by a particular tradition that attracts you.

Deciding whether or not to ask your friends to read portions of the service is not always easy. On the one hand, couples would like to see as many of their friends as possible involved in their wedding as a way of sharing their joy; and many parishes today, eager to encourage active participation in the liturgy, encourage couples to find their own lectors. On the other hand, having lay lectors can be mildly disruptive, especially when they are seated with the rest of the congregation or are not proficient in public reading. Traditionally, in those churches with an ordained ministry, either the priest or a duly ordained lector wearing vestments would proclaim the Scriptures, while the friends and family of the couple would participate liturgically in other ways: as groomsmen, bridesmaids, witnesses, gift-bearers, or *patroni* (sponsors) who crown or veil the bride and groom (see Chapter V). Indeed, rediscovering nuptial traditions creates more opportunities for loved ones to take an active part in your wedding.

ALLOCUTIONS

Choosing an allocution can also be a delicate matter. Since most pastors are used to composing their own sermons, some may take umbrage at being given a "script" to read, as it could easily appear to them that you have no faith in their talent or are implying that you know more about the topic than they do. Broach this topic with considerable tact, as it is not a common request to make. An unvetted or spontaneous sermon has the advantage of delight and surprise (provided that it has a good message and is full of verve), but it has the disadvantage of dragging the service down if the sermon has too much length or too little quality. Choosing your own allocution, on the other hand, guarantees a relatively brief exhortation or homily that is pleasing to you, but it precludes the possibility of learning something new from the homilist and also runs the risk of offending him. Perhaps an agreeable compromise would be to suggest an allocution to a presider as a rough template, asking that some of its elements be incorporated into the homily.

If you are allowed to choose an allocution on your own, try to harmonize your selection with your Bible readings. Be attentive to biblical references in the allocution; perhaps you may wish to find the corresponding passages for your readings. This advice also applies to the pastors or homilists consulting *Wedding Rites,* who are of course free to use an entire allocution verbatim or to lift passages from several sources and weave them, along with their own thoughts, into a new whole.

Finally, both pastors and couples must bear in mind that there are either one or two specific times in the marriage service where a presider is to speak to the couple. If there are no readings during the service, there is no homily; and if there is no homily, the opening address or allocution at the beginning serves as the main vehicle for instructing and inspiring the couple. If there are readings, however, the pastor's remarks should be distributed between the opening address and the homily, with greater emphasis being placed on the latter. Most of the allocutions found in this chapter were originally used as the opening address, but they can, with a little adaptation, be used for the homily as well.

IV. Vows

Let me not to the marriage of true minds
Admit impediments. Love is not love
Which alters when it alteration finds,
Or bends with the remover to remove:
O, no! it is an ever-fixed mark,
That looks on tempests and is never shaken;
It is the star to every wandering bark,
Whose worth's unknown, although his height be taken.
Love's not Time's fool, though rosy lips and cheeks
Within his bending sickle's compass come;
Love alters not with his brief hours and weeks,
But bears it out even to the edge of doom,
If this be error, and upon me prov'd,
I never writ, nor man ever lov'd.

Shakespeare,
Sonnet CXVI

PAGEANTRY AND SPECTACLE enrich our enjoyment and our memory of weddings, yet the essence of the wedding itself is simple and unassuming: a brief recitation, made freely and from the heart, taking less than a minute to say but being enough to change one's life forever. The vow is not merely an exchange of words — it is the core of the nuptial event, setting the terms on which a man and a woman begin their new life together as one.

Among the many treasures we were thrilled to discover in the course of researching this book are a number of French vows from the Middle Ages. These are among the earliest recorded vows we have, though it is their flavor rather than their age which makes them so interesting. The vows speak unapologetically of conjugal intimacy, referring frequently to the body without any sign of self-consciousness. One vow, which we mention only here, even contains a pledge to be "bonere and buxome in bedde and at borde"! Yet the vows nevertheless refer to sexual matters with taste and subtlety. They are ideal, then, for a couple wishing to have solemn tradition but not Victorian prudery.

Something else that impresses us about these vows is the strength of their commitment. Admittedly, some of them border on the comical. A vow from eastern France in the 1500s, for example, contains the pledge: "I will never abandon thee for another who is more beautiful, more sweet, more pious, or even more virtuous."* Yet another from Paris in the 1300s promises that "I will never replace thee with another, nor cast thee out, all the days of my life." By articulating the seductive alternatives to marital fidelity and then soundly rejecting them, however, these vows have the merit of making the couple aware of the moral dangers they face.

Medieval vows are far from being the only impressive specimens of their kind from the treasury of tradition. The second section of this chapter will provide a variety of vows from the Renaissance and beyond. Afterwards, we will present the prototype of all Western weddings, the Jewish contract. Finally, we will offer suggestions on how to sort through this wealth of options.

---

* Why the "thou's" and "thee's" in traditional prayers and vows? Contrary to what many think, "thou" is the English pronoun that expresses intimacy and familiarity, while "you" is used on formal occasions or for one's superior (it is also the plural form of "thou"). That God is addressed with "Thou" in the Scriptures suggests, among other things, the surprising intimacy between God and His people, despite God's obvious superiority.

A Selection of Medieval French Vows

BARBEAU

This earthy set of vows from the 1100s establishes a pattern which will be widely followed.

P. N., say after me:

M. N., I take thee as my wife and my spouse, and so I join thee in faith to my body, that I may bring thee faithfully and loyally to my body and my belongings; and so I will keep thee in health and in sickness and in whatever state that Our Lord deigns thee to be in, and neither for better nor for worse will I replace thee with another, all the days of my life.

P. N., say after me:

W. N., I take thee as my husband and my spouse, and so I join thee in faith to my body, that I may bring thee faithfully and loyally to my body and my belongings; and so I will keep thee in health and in sickness and in whatever state that Our Lord deigns thee to be in, and neither for better nor for worse will I replace thee with another, all the days of my life.

ROUEN

In these vows from the 1200s, notice the use of the word "indeed," as if to say, "Are you sure you want to go through with this?"

P. Dost thou indeed want N. for thy wife, to keep her in sickness and in health all the days of thy life — as an upright man ought to keep his wife — and to make faithful fellowship with her in body and belongings?

M. I do.

P. Dost thou indeed want N. for thy husband, to keep him in sickness and in health all the days of thy life — as an upright woman ought to keep her husband — and to make faithful fellowship with him in body and belongings?

W.   I do.

MEAUX

Note the dramatic yet quaint quality of the pastor's question: "Dost thou receive him thus?" This rite, from 1280, is the only one we encountered where the woman is addressed before the man.

P.   N., dost thou wish to have N. as thy husband and spouse?

W.   I do.

P.   N., dost thou wish to have N. as thy wife and spouse?

M.   I do.

They join their right hands.

P.   N., I hand N. over to thee as husband and spouse, that thou may keep him in sickness and in health, and that thou may serve him faithfully according to the precepts of the Church. Dost thou receive him thus?

W.   I do.

P.   N., I hand N. over to thee as wife and spouse, that thou may keep her in sickness and in health, and that thou may serve her faithfully according to the precepts of the Church. Dost thou receive her thus?

M.   I do.

P.   In the name of the Father, and of the Son, ✠ and of the Holy Spirit. Amen.

PARIS

One of the most striking sets of vows (from the 1200s) in both its beauty and in its level of commitment is the following. What else would one expect from Paris during the century that saw the cathedral of Notre Dame completed?

P.　N., dost thou promise in the sight of God that thou wilt keep N. as thy wife: that thou wilt have her and hold her in faith and fidelity, in health and in sickness, and in all other misfortunes: and that either for better or for worse, thou wilt not replace her with another, nor cast her out, all the days of thy life?

W.　I do.

P.　N., dost thou promise in the sight of God that thou wilt keep N. as thy husband: that thou wilt have him and hold him in faith and fidelity, in health and in sickness, and in all other misfortunes: and that either for better or for worse, thou wilt not replace him with another, nor cast him out, all the days of thy life?

M.　I do.

CAMBRAI

This rite from the 1300s is unusual for having the presentation of the ring take place in between the exchange of vows. Note the strength of the pledges.

M.　N., with my body I thee honor, and with this silver (or gold) I thee endow, and all that I have and will have I give and will give to thee in faithful fellowship and companionship. And I promise thee, here and before God, that I will carry thee in faith and loyalty, in health and in sickness, and in all the states that God might put thee; and that I will take care of thee, even as I do myself. And I will never abandon thee for another, so long as we both shall live.

He puts the ring on her finger.

W.   N., I take thee as my husband and my spouse. And all that I have
      and will have, that I have acquired and can acquire, I give and will
      give to thee in faithful fellowship and companionship. And I prom-
      ise thee, here and before God, that I will carry thee in faith and loy-
      alty, in health and in sickness, and in all the states that God might
      put thee; and that I will take care of thee, even as I do myself. And I
      will never abandon thee for another, so long as we both shall live.

Avignon

This brief tête-à-tête from the 1300s almost has the quality of a Shake-
spearean romantic comedy and is definitely one of the more unusual sets
of vows we came upon.

M.   I give to thee my body as spouse and husband.

W.   I give to thee my body as wife.

M.   And I receive thee as my wife.

W.   And I receive thee as my husband.

Paris (2)

Here is another unusual set of vows, also from the 1300s. Notice the
prominent role of the priest, and the down-to-earth character of the
lines.

P.   Brother, wilt thou have this woman N. to wife?

M.   I will.

P.   I therefore give her to thee that thou may keep her, in sickness and
      in health, as thy lawful wife, and that thou may bring her into faith-
      ful fellowship, as our Lord God commands, as Saint Paul teaches,
      and as Holy Church holds. Dost thou agree to this?

M.   I do.

P.	Sister, wilt thou have this man N. to husband?

W.	I will.

P.	I therefore give him to thee that thou may keep him, in sickness and in health, as thy lawful husband, and that thou may bring him into faithful fellowship, as our Lord God commands, as Saint Paul teaches, and as Holy Church holds. Dost thou agree to this?

W.	I do.

A Selection of Vows from the Renaissance and Beyond

The vows following the Middle Ages did not so much depart from their predecessors as develop them. Protestant Reformers, for example, wished to modify certain Catholic teachings on marriage but kept many of the features of the medieval vow intact. We have included a number of vows from the mid-1500s to the turn of the last century, especially those used in the United States. If you do not see your particular denomination, consult the Advice section of this chapter.

ROMAN CATHOLIC (TRIDENTINE)*

This format, which was prescribed in the Catholic Church from the late 1500s until the 1960s and is still available today, is interesting for a couple of reasons. First, the clause in the initial question about taking one's spouse "according to the rite of our Holy Mother the Church" implies that the whole service, not just the sermon, is designed to celebrate and teach the essence of marriage — a conviction, incidentally, that undergirds this book. Second, unlike other practices, the priest declares the man and the woman married before the exchange of the rings as a way

---

* The Tridentine rite, which is named after the Council of Trent (1545-63), was used by the Catholic Church from 1570 until 1965. (Most elements of the rite, however, are centuries older.) Now called the extraordinary form of the Roman rite, it is available upon request to every Catholic couple (see *Summorum Pontificum*, Art. 5, §3).

of emphasizing that these tokens do not make the state of marriage but symbolize it.

P.   N., wilt thou take N. here present for thy lawful wife, according to the rite of our Holy Mother the Church?

W.   I will.

P.   N., wilt thou take N. here present for thy lawful husband, according to the rite of our Holy Mother the Church?

W.   I will.

M.   I, N., take thee, N., for my lawful wife, to have and to hold, from this day forward, for better, for worse, for richer, for poorer, in sickness and in health, until death do us part.*

W.   I, N., take thee, N., for my lawful husband, to have and to hold, from this day forward, for better, for worse, for richer, for poorer, in sickness and in health, until death do us part.*

P.   I join you together in matrimony. In the name of the Father, and of the Son, ✠ and of the Holy Spirit. Amen.

ANGLICAN

This careful alteration of a medieval Catholic English rite in 1549 (note the similarities to the vow above) became the model for later Anglican, Episcopalian, American Presbyterian, and American Methodist vows.

P.   N., wilt thou have this woman to thy wedded wife, to live together after God's ordinance in the holy estate of matrimony? Wilt thou love her, comfort her, honour, and keep her, in sickness and in health? And forsaking all other, keep thee only to her, so long as you both shall live?

* In some places "and thereto I plight thee my troth" is added as the final clause.

The man shall answer:

I will.

Then shall the Priest say to the woman:

N., wilt thou have this man to thy wedded husband, to live together after God's ordinance, in the holy estate of matrimony? Wilt thou obey him, and serve him, love, honour, and keep him, in sickness and in health? And forsaking all other, keep thee only to him, so long as you both shall live?

The woman shall answer:

I will.

Then shall the Priest say:

Who giveth this woman to be married unto this man?

And the Priest receiving the woman at her father, or friend's hands, shall cause the man to take the woman by the right hand, and so either to give their troth to other, the man first saying:

M.   I, N., take thee, N., to my wedded wife, to have and to hold, from this day forward, for better, for worse, for richer, for poorer, in sickness, and in health, to love and to cherish, till death us depart: according to God's holy ordinance, and thereto I plight thee my troth.

Then they shall loose their hands, and the woman taking again the man by the right hand, shall say:

W.   I, N., take thee, N., to my wedded husband, to have and to hold, from this day forward, for better, for worse, for richer, for poorer, in sickness, and in health, to love, cherish, and to obey, till death us depart, according to God's holy ordinance: and thereto I give thee my troth.

EPISCOPALIAN

The Episcopalian vows from the 1790 *Book of Common Prayer,* which became the primary model for many American Protestant denominations, are identical to the Anglican except for the use of "till death us do part" near the end.

LUTHERAN

In his 1542 Marriage Service, Luther strove to cover the essence of matrimony without undue flourish. His succinct vows, unceremonious exchange of rings, and simple declaration of marriage met his objective admirably. In keeping with medieval custom, the vows would be exchanged at the door of the church, followed by the allocution and blessing inside at the altar.

P.   N., dost thou desire N. to thy wedded wife?

M.   Yes.

P.   N., does thou desire N. to thy wedded husband?

W.   Yes.

They exchange rings and join their right hands. The pastor then says to them:

P.   What God hath joined together, let not man put asunder. Since N. and N. desire each other in marriage and acknowledge the same here publicly before God and the world, in testimony of which they have given each other their hands and wedding rings, I pronounce them joined in marriage. In the name of the Father and of the Son and of the Holy Spirit. Amen.

CALVINIST

The earliest followers of John Calvin had this rite straight from the master's pen. Notice the greater emphasis on the congregation.

P.   You, therefore, N. and N., knowing that God hath ordained things thus, do you wish to live in the holy estate of matrimony, which God hath so greatly honored? Have you such a purpose, as you bear witness here before this holy assembly, asking that it be approved?

R.   Yes.

P.   I address you who are present here as witnesses, entreating you to remember: if there is anyone who knows of some impediment, or that either of them is linked to another in marriage, let him say so.

If no one speaks, the pastor continues:

Then, because there is no one who objects and no impediment, may our Lord God confirm your holy purpose, which He hath given you; and may your beginning be in the name of God, who made heaven and earth. Amen.

Dost thou, N., confess here before God and His holy congregation, that thou hast taken and dost take for thy wife and spouse, N., here present: that thou dost promise to keep her, loving her and holding her faithfully, as a true and faithful husband ought to; and that thou wilt live in holiness with her, keeping faith and loyalty to her in all things, according to the holy word of God and His holy gospel?

M.   Yes.

P.   Dost thou, N., confess here before God and His holy congregation, that thou hast taken and dost take N. for thy lawful husband, whom thou dost promise to obey, serving him and being subject to him, living in holiness with him, keeping faith and loyalty to him in all things, as a faithful and loyal wife ought to, according to the word of God and His holy gospel?

W. Yes.

P. May the Father of all mercy, who out of His grace hath called you
    to this holy estate of matrimony, through the love of Jesus Christ
    His Son, who by His holy presence sanctified marriage and made it
    the first miracle before His Apostles, give you His Holy Spirit, that
    you may serve and honor Him in this noble estate. Amen.

PRESBYTERIAN

The Presbyterian church in the U.S. at the turn of the last century em-
ployed this set of vows:

P. N., wilt thou have this woman to be thy wife, and wilt thou pledge
    thy troth to her, in all love and honour, in all duty and service, in all
    faith and tenderness, to live with her, and cherish her, according to
    the ordinances of God, in the holy bond of Marriage?

M. I will.

P. N., wilt thou have this man to be thy husband, and wilt thou
    pledge thy troth to him, in all love and honour, in all duty and ser-
    vice, in all faith and tenderness, to live with him, and cherish him,
    according to the ordinances of God, in the holy bond of Marriage?

W. I will.

P. Who giveth this Woman to be married to this Man?

    *The father puts her hand in the minister's, who in turn places it in the
    man's.*

M. I, N., take thee, N., to be my wedded wife: and I do promise and
    covenant, before God and these witnesses, to be thy loving and
    faithful husband, in plenty and in want, in joy and in sorrow, in sick-
    ness and in health, as long as we both shall live.

The woman then takes the man's hand and says:

I, N., take thee, N., to be my wedded husband: and I do promise and covenant, before God and these witnesses, to be thy loving and faithful wife, in plenty and in want, in joy and in sorrow, in sickness and in health, as long as we both shall live.

QUAKER

At some point in an ordinary nineteenth-century weekday meeting of the Society of Friends, the man and woman would stand up and take each other's hand. Then the man would say something like:

Friends, I take this my friend, N., to be my wife, promising through divine assistance, to be unto her a loving and faithful husband, until it shall please the Lord by death to separate us.

The woman then says:

Friends, I take this my friend, N., to be my husband, promising through divine assistance, to be unto him a loving and faithful wife, until it shall please the Lord by death to separate us.

The Declaration of Marriage

Many of the vows we have examined put the official declaration of marriage after the ring ceremony or simply do not have it at all. For those who would like more of a conclusion, we suggest this statement for the pastor from sixteenth-century Germany.

May God confirm the marriage contracted between you. And I solemnize it in the presence of the Church. In the name of the Father, and of the Son, ✠ and of the Holy Spirit. Amen.

The Jewish Marriage Contract, or *Ketubah*

The Jewish *ketubah,* which has been in existence since the first century A.D., is not a contract made directly between bride and groom but a legal document confirmed by two witnesses in which the groom promises to take his bride to wife under the conditions stipulated. The *ketubah* is signed immediately before the wedding service; it is then read aloud and handed over to the bride following the *kiddushin* (the "betrothal," or first part of the ceremony). From that point on it is hers to keep as a perpetual guarantee of her rights and her husband's duties to her.

Though many different kinds of *ketubot* have arisen since the 1970s, the only one that is recognized as valid under Jewish law is the traditional *ketubah.* Written in Aramaic, it has changed little since the 200s. We include here an English translation.

> **Happiness and Prosperity!**
> **The Voice of Mirth, and the Voice of Gladness;**
> **The Voice of the Bridegroom, and the Voice of the Bride.**
>
> On [such a] day, [such a] month, [such a] year, counted from the creation of the world, according to the reckoning which are accustomed to use here in the city of _____ in the land of [North America].
>
> I, the bridegroom N., son of N., said to this N., here present, daughter of N., "Be to me for a wife according to the law of Moses and Israel. Then will I cherish, honor, sustain and maintain thee, according to the custom of Jewish husbands, who cherish, honor, sustain and maintain their wives in fidelity; and I lay down for thee [so many dollars] due to thee [by law, or by agreement, etc.]; and I will feed and clothe thee and supply thy wants, and treat thee as husband in private, according to the custom of every land.
>
> And the honored bride, N., daughter of R. [a chaste virgin or widow, etc.], was willing to be his wife. Moreover the dowry which she brought, whether in silver or gold, jewelry, ornaments and clothing, or in immovable property, was estimated at [so many dollars]. And the honored N., son of N., the bridegroom here present,

added to her, of his own [property, or expectations], [so many dollars], making in all [so many dollars] in silver.

And N., son of N., the bridegroom here present, said as follows: "The guaranty of this marriage-contract and this addition, I take on me and on my heirs after me, to be paid from the best real estate and other property that belongs to me under the heaven, which I have acquired and which I shall acquire in the future. Such real estate and other property as has any encumbrance, and that which has none, shall be pledged and bound to pay from them this marriage-contract and its addition, even from the cloak of my shoulder, in life and in death, from this day and forever."

And the guaranty of this marriage-contract and its addition, N., son of N., the bridegroom here present, took on himself with all the severity of marriage-contracts and their additions which are used with the daughters of Israel, made according to the rules of our sages (Blessed be they!), and not like unimportant or common contracts and acquisitions. All, as is written and explained above, is in full force from N., son of N., the bridegroom here present, to the honored N., daughter of N., this bride here present, by it all duly and properly to acquire.

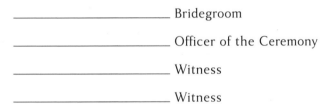

_____ Bridegroom

_____ Officer of the Ceremony

_____ Witness

_____ Witness

Advice

Choosing a vow will depend a great deal on your religious affiliation or convictions about marriage. Whether you consider marriage a sacrament, a contract, or an "estate," or what role you think the church plays in facilitating your marriage, will affect your decision. Our advice is to get together with your betrothed and go through these vows carefully and slowly. As we said at the beginning of this chapter, vows are not simply words, but the terms under which you wish to live your lives together. They should be taken seriously.

If you are a Protestant Christian and do not see your own denomination represented, it is possible that your church traditionally used the Anglican or Episcopalian vows. Many American denominations, as we have mentioned before, did not prescribe any one formula but as a matter of course followed the 1790 Episcopalian service book. (This is why its lines are so familiar to Americans of all faiths.) If you are a Byzantine-rite Christian, you probably already know that there are no explicit vows in the nuptial liturgy. Several Byzantine Catholic churches, however, sometimes include declarations of consent and marriage vows in their services, while a Greek Orthodox priest will privately confirm that the couple has come here freely with the intent of getting married before the service begins. For the moment when the two become one in a Byzantine marriage, see the Crowning ceremony in the next chapter.

If you are a Jew looking for a *ketubah,* the first place to go is to your rabbi, who will most likely have a number of pre-made copies. Bear in mind, however, that although the content of this document is strictly regulated, its form is not. Historically *ketubot* have taken many different shapes and sizes, reflecting the artistic and cultural tastes of different times and climes. Today professionally calligraphed *ketubot* are available for the well-off and lithographs and prints for the more economically minded. You and your fiancée are even free to draft your own *ketubah.* *Ketubot* should not be pretentious, but it is considered a pious obligation to make them as beautiful as possible. In addition to your rabbi, Judaica shops are an excellent source for ideas.

V. Ceremonies

May her bridegroom bring her to a house
Where all's accustomed, ceremonious;
For arrogance and hatred are the wares
Peddled in the thoroughfares.
How but in custom and in ceremony
Are innocence and beauty born?
Ceremony's a name for the rich horn,
And custom for the spreading laurel tree.

W. B. Yeats,
"A Prayer for My Daughter"

T HE INNOCENCE AND BEAUTY of ceremony shine no more
clearly than in a traditional wedding. From the Jewish breaking of
the cup to the Byzantine crowning, nuptial ceremonies quietly
sing of the greatness of married life. Marriage services can, of course, be
simple to the point of Spartan. But when couples draw from the rich
symbolism and ceremonial splendor of their religious and ethnic traditions, so much more of the *joy* of marriage is captured in their weddings.
Ceremonies, as poets like Yeats well knew, enrich our lives; they help us

learn the true meaning of an event, and they sharpen our memory so that we won't ever forget that meaning. In this chapter we will meet many ceremonies, some well known, some rare, and hear advice on how to incorporate them into a contemporary wedding.

Despite the enormous variety of customs surrounding weddings, the traditions which are a formal part of the service can be divided into four simple categories: those which pertain to the head, the lips, the fingers, and the hand. We will begin at the top and work our way down.

Sacred Coverings

The custom of covering the couple's heads during the marriage ceremony is a cross-cultural phenomenon stretching back many centuries. In the Jewish ceremony a *chuppah*, or bridal canopy, hovers over the heads of the couple on four poles. In the Byzantine rite, the coronation of the couple with two special crowns defines the moment that a couple is married. And among Western Christians the wedding veil, or carecloth, would once be placed on the shoulders of the couple or held over their heads during the most important nuptial blessing. Each of these traditions offers a different rationale for its custom, so it is difficult to say why the head covering is so ubiquitous throughout the world. Our speculation is that the physical act of putting on a new garment somehow translates into the notion of "putting on" a new life in marriage, while putting this garment on or near the head further underlines the dignity of marriage (the head being viewed as the most dignified part of the body). Whatever their origins, sacred coverings are certainly stunning; they arrest the attention of the congregation and convey a sense of awe and mystery.

THE *CHUPPAH*

For many the first thing that comes to mind when they think of a Jewish wedding is the image of a couple standing under the bridal canopy, or *chuppah*. It is thought that when Jewish marriages moved from the home to the synagogue, the *chuppah* was invented to represent the former. (It has also been said that it represents God's presence and Abraham's tent.) In any case, the couple stands under it during the entire ceremony, as they and their guests praise the Lord "who sanctifieth Israel with the bridal canopy and the sacred marriage rites." The *chuppah,* which can come in any color, is typically made of a heavy cloth square (four feet by four feet) connected to a long pole at each corner. Its edges can be ornate and gilded, as can the pattern (e.g., the Star of David) that may be sewn onto the center. There are, however, no laws regulating the dimensions or designs of *chuppahs,* and so you are encouraged to consider a number of options or to even make your own.

Mention should also be made of an additional custom among Sephardic Jews of putting on a *tallit,* or prayer shawl, over the heads of the bride and groom during the nuptial blessings. The *tallit* is used for all kinds of solemn prayer, but in this context it represents the holiness of the event and a public affirmation to live by the Mosaic law.

THE CARECLOTH

The couple's wedding veil, or carecloth, was once so important in the Western imagination that it literally gave the wedding event its name. When a woman in ancient Rome was married, she put on a fiery red veil as a sign of the new obligations and dignity she was taking on as a matron. In Latin this act of covering oneself with a veil was known as *nubere,* from which comes our word "nuptial." Latin Christians adopted the veil in the 300s (or perhaps earlier) but put the man under it as well to stress the fact that *both* bride and groom were expected to live up to their marital obligations. This explains why it came to be called a carecloth in English, as "to care" once meant "to lay a burden on." After the Renaissance, the carecloth was itself overshadowed by the bridal veil in most parts of Europe (a pale substitute, in our humble opinion), though it continues to be used in several areas of the world today.

The carecloth is a linen or silk sheet smaller than a *chuppah* and rectangular. It is usually white with either a red pattern on it or with a red cord attached to it. According the St. Isidore of Seville (d. 636), the white symbolizes the purity of Christian marital love and the red the continuation of one's family blood-line.

The carecloth is classically used during the Solemn Nuptial Blessing of the Mass (see Chapter VI) in two different ways. In one use, it is draped over the shoulders of the groom and over the head and shoulders of the bride as they kneel for the blessing. In this case it signifies the yoke of marriage joining them together. But the carecloth can also be suspended over the heads of the kneeling couple by the best man and maid of honor, by two altar servers, or by two specially designated sponsors (each holding a side). In this case, because it partially hides the couple from view, it reminds them to refrain from untoward public displays of affection and to keep family matters confidential. In former ages this custom also served another purpose: If the couple had produced an offspring out of wedlock, placing the child under the carecloth with the parents would automatically render him or her legitimate!

Though the carecloth is a gem to which all Western Christians, Catholic or Protestant, can lay equal claim, it is particularly popular in the Philippines, where it remains an integral part of the wedding ceremony. Commonly referred to as the couple's "wedding veil," the Filipino *velo* is made of white tulle (no doubt a prudent adaptation to the islands' steamy climate) and is placed onto the groom's shoulders and the bride's head by two specially designated veil sponsors (a *ninong* and *ninang*). It is said that the veil draped in this way represents the bride and groom or their families becoming one, as well as hope for the couple's health and protection. After the veil is pinned in place, another pair of sponsors places the cord, or *yugal*, in the shape of a figure eight over the heads of the couple to symbolize the infinite bond of married love. The *yugal*, incidentally, is usually a white silk rope, though it can also be made of flowers, links of coins, or even diamonds.

A related tradition among Mexicans and Mexican-Americans is the joining of a couple with a *lazo* (a large set of double-looped rosary beads) instead of a veil or carecloth. This pious option, which is likewise carried out by a pair of elder sponsors, or *padrinos,* vividly captures the binding of man and woman together in holy wedlock.

THE CROWNING

Like the carecloth, the Christian crown finds its roots in pagan custom.*
Interestingly enough, crowns have never been a liturgical component of
Roman Catholic or Protestant weddings, though they have always been a
part of the European bridal costume, either in the form of a wreath or as
garlands in the hair or as an exquisite tiara. This is especially true in eastern Europe, where a bride would traditionally be "crowned" and given a
shawl to wear during the ritual procession from her home to the church.
(After the service, her crown would be removed and replaced by the head-
dress betokening a married woman.) And it is equally true in Scandinavian
countries, where great bridal crowns, wrought in gold or silver and
adorned with jewels or charms, are handed down from one generation to
the next. (The Lutheran churches in these areas, incidentally, have cherished this custom as much as the Catholic.) There are also charming superstitions which have originated from the bridal crown. In Finland, a garland of flowers replaces the bouquet toss as the means of predicting who
will be the next bride. The bride is blindfolded, and while her maidens circle around her, she places the garland on one of their lucky heads. In Swit-
zerland, on the other hand, the bridal wreath is burned after the ceremony, and if it does so quickly, the new bride is ensured good luck.

But it was left to the Byzantine Christians from Greece and the Slavic
lands to make good use of this old practice within the liturgy itself. Since the
300s the crown has been used in the Byzantine rite as an integral part of the
wedding service. It is so important, in fact, that just as the carecloth gave
Western weddings the word "nuptial," Byzantine wedding ceremonies are
simply referred to as "crownings." Symbolizing the couple's chaste triumph
over lust, their "enthronement" as king and queen of their new home, and
their martyrdom to selfishness and egotism, the crowns can be made of flowers, silk, or metal and are usually connected to each other by a long white
ribbon. At the appropriate point in the service, either the priest or the sponsors place the crowns on the heads of the couple, an act that in Orthodox
Christianity more or less constitutes the moment they become one in marriage. The following is the Byzantine coronation of the wedding pair:

* For the Jewish crown, see the Flowers section of Chapter II, p. 37.

The priest begins with a prayer:

O God, who art holy, who didst fashion man from the ground, and build up woman from his rib, and join to him a help meet for him, because it so pleased Thy majesty that man should not be alone upon the earth: Do Thou also now, O Sovereign Master, put forth Thy hand from Thy holy habitation, and join Thy servant, this N., here present and Thy handmaid, this N. here present, because of Thee is woman joined to man. Join them together in harmony: unite them by the crown into one flesh; vouchsafe to them fruit of the womb, and the delight of goodly offspring. For Thine is the might, and Thine is the kingdom and the power and the glory, the Father and the Son and the Holy Spirit, now and always, even for ever and ever. Amen.

The priest, taking the crown, puts it on the head of the man, and says three times:

The servant of God, N., is crowned with the handmaid of God, this N., here present, in the name of the Father, and of the Son, ✠ and of the Holy Spirit. Amen.

He makes the sign of the cross. Then, taking the second crown, he puts it on the head of the woman, saying three times:

The handmaid of God, N., is crowned with the servant of God, this N. here present, in the name of the Father, and of the Son, ✠ and of the Holy Spirit. Amen.

He makes the sign of the cross. Then he blesses them, saying three times:

O Lord our God, crown them with glory and honor.

THE UNCROWNING

The Byzantine liturgy also has a ceremony for the removal of the crowns at the end of the service. As the priest removes the man's crown, he says:

Be magnified, O bridegroom, as Abraham, and be blessed as Isaac, and be multiplied as Jacob, walking in peace, and doing in righteousness the commandments of God.

As he removes the woman's crown, he says:

And thou, O bride, be magnified as Sarah, and be delighted as Rebecca, and be multiplied as Rachel, delighting in thine own husband and observing the boundaries of the law, for so has it pleased God.

Then the deacon says:

Of the Lord let us make entreaty.

And the priest responds with the following prayer:

O God our God, who wast present in Cana of Galilee, and didst bless the marriage there, bless also these Thy servants, who by Thy providence have been joined together into the society of marriage. Bless their going in and coming out; fill their life with good things; receive their crowns in Thine own kingdom, and preserve them from spot, fault, and adulterous snares, for ever and ever. Amen.

The Loving Cup

Another similarity between Jewish and Christian ceremonies is the sharing of a cup. This is usually associated with Jewish weddings because of the unforgettable act of smashing the cup after it is used, but the cup is also a part of the Byzantine marriage service and of Western Christianity's nuptial festivities. Because of the obvious symbolism of two drinking from the same cup, its popularity is understandable.

JEWISH

There are actually two cups used in the Jewish wedding: one during the betrothal ceremony *(kiddushin)* and one at the conclusion of the service.

While the tradition of smashing the cup at the end has come to symbolize many things (including the destruction of the Temple in Jerusalem, the frailty of life, and the irrevocability of marriage), its origin is attributed to Mar, son of Ravina, who was concerned about the growing high spirits of several rabbis at a wedding. Taking an expensive cup, he broke it in front of them in order to quell their exuberance. It worked.

Before the first cup is drunk, the following three benedictions (the birkat erusin*) are said in Hebrew by the presiding rabbi:*

Blessed art Thou, O Lord our God, King of the universe, who hast created the fruit of the wine!

Blessed art Thou, O Lord our God, King of the universe, who hast sanctified us with Thy commandments, and hast forbidden us fornication, and hast restrained us from the betrothed, but hast permitted us those who are married to us by means of the canopy and sacred rites.

Blessed art Thou, O Lord, who sanctifiest Israel by means of the bridal canopy and sacred marriage rites.

The rabbi then tastes the wine and gives the cup to the bridegroom and bride, who also drink from it.

The second cup is drunk after the marriage contract has been signed. The presiding rabbi first says the blessing (again, see Chapter VI), drinks from the cup, and then gives it to the man and woman, inviting them to do the same. The cup is then placed in a handkerchief and crushed under the groom's heel. A shout of "Mazel Tov!" — Congratulations! — concludes the service.

Byzantine

In Byzantine weddings, after the "Our Father" is recited, the priest blesses a chalice filled with wine called the common cup. He then says the following prayer:

O God, who hast made all things by Thy power and established the habitable earth, set in order the crown of all things that have been made by Thee, and granted this cup of fellowship to those who have been joined into the society of marriage, bless it with a spiritual blessing. For blessed is Thy name, and glorified is Thy kingdom, the Father, and the Son, and the Holy Spirit, now and always, even for ever and ever. Amen.

The priest takes the cup and gives it three times, first to the man, then to the woman. After this he has them follow him in a circle while an anthem is sung (see Circling below).

WESTERN CHRISTIAN

Like the crown, the loving cup never made its way into the Western marriage service proper, though it was used extensively at wedding feasts. For more on loving cups in the Roman Catholic and Protestant traditions (including a blessing), see Chapter VII.

Circling

In addition to the use of a cup, Judaism and Byzantine Christianity also have incorporated into their liturgies the ritual act of making a circle. In Byzantine Catholic and Eastern Orthodox churches this takes place immediately after taking the common cup. The priest takes an icon of Christ and walks three times in a circle while the man and woman follow him, in order that their first steps together as a married couple might be in the footsteps of Christ and to signify their transition to a nobler state of life.* Judaism, on the other hand, has the custom of the bride walking in a circle around the groom before they enter the *chuppah* or at some other point in the ceremony. She may do this three times or seven, either alone or accompanied by both mothers of the couple, depending on the tradition being followed. The number three is considered significant because it

---

* Among Slavic Byzantines the circling takes place around the icon-table, or tetrapod, accompanied by a beautiful refrain that begins with the words, "Dance, Isaiah!"

is the number of betrothals binding God to His people Israel (q.v. Hosea 2:21-22), while the number seven ties into the days of creation.

The Ring

If there is any one symbol of marriage, it is the ring. Originally a ring was given to a maiden to signify a man's intention to marry her. The Romans, for example, would give their betrothed an iron ring as a part of the pre-nuptial arrangement. The ring was also seen as a token of the man's *dower* — the portion of his estate that his wife was guaranteed to have after he died.

But the ring quickly came to mean much more. The simple iron ring of the Romans became the precious gold or silver ring of Christians and Jews, a telling indication of how dear marriage is in these religions. The circular shape of the ring came to symbolize the eternity of the couple's love for each other, while the jewels represented the quality and character of that love. In fact, a whole lexicon of meaning has been built around each jewel.

More importantly, the ring became a part of marriage as well as of betrothal. Simple gold or silver bands advertised to the world that this woman — and, much later, this man — were forever changed by the yoke of marriage. As Jeremy Taylor wrote in 1653, the marriage ring signifies "the union of hands and hearts." Originally the ring was worn on the more dignified hand, the right, to signify the honor of marriage; and in fact many European countries retain this custom. Since the Renaissance, however, the English and a number of others have worn the ring on the fourth finger of the left hand, as it was believed at the time that a vein went from this finger directly to the heart. The custom still remains, despite the change in scientific opinion.

If the ring is the symbol *par excellence* of marriage, it is not surprising that it came to have a prominent place in the wedding ritual. The blessing, followed by the giving of the ring, is the most enduring of all marriage customs and the ultimate seal on the union that has just been made. It is not surprising that playful superstitions have arisen around this memorable event: It was said, for example, that if the husband had any difficulty slipping the ring on his wife's finger, he would not be able to handle her!

And, of course, it is not surprising that words are spoken as well, both by the pastor and by the couple. In fact, the ring ceremony gives us some of the most beautiful prayers of the pastor, and some of the raciest lines of the couple. Consider the medieval and Renaissance English verse, "With this ring I thee wed, and with this body I thee worship."

BLESSING THE RING

Roman Catholic (Tridentine)

Latin Christianity's love for dialogue and for the Psalms are both reflected in this plaintive opening by the priest and his respondents — the servers, the choir, the congregation, or the couple. This ritual follows the ancient custom of giving a wedding ring only to the bride, though this can be amended to meet today's practices.

The priest begins with several verses from the Psalms:

P. Our help is in the name of the Lord.

R. Who made heaven and earth.

P. O Lord, hear my prayer.

R. And let my cry come before Thee.

P. The Lord be with you.

R. And with thy spirit.

The priest then says:

Let us pray.

Bless, O Lord, this ring, which we bless in Thy name: that she who is to wear it may, in rendering unbroken faith to her spouse, ever abide in Thy peace and in Thy will; and may she always live with him in mutual love. Through Christ our Lord. Amen.

He then sprinkles the ring with holy water in the form of a cross.

Medieval

These prayers, used throughout Europe by Catholics during the Middle Ages, were probably included in a format similar to the one above.

- Creator and Preserver of mankind, Giver of spiritual grace, eternal God: permit the Holy Spirit the Paraclete to be upon this ring. Through our Lord Jesus Christ Thy Son, who liveth and reigneth with Thee in the unity of the Holy Spirit, God, forever and ever. Amen.
- Bless, O Lord, this ring which we bless in Thy name, that she who wears it may dwell in Thy peace, live in Thy love, and grow old and be multiplied unto length of days. Through our Lord Jesus Christ Thy Son, who liveth and reigneth with Thee in the unity of the Holy Spirit, God, forever and ever. Amen.
- Creator and Preserver of mankind, Giver of spiritual grace, Bestower of eternal salvation: send Thou, O Lord, Thy Spirit the Paraclete upon this ring, that she who wears it may be armed in the strength of a heavenly defense, and may it profit her unto eternal salvation. Through our Lord Jesus Christ Thy Son, who liveth and reigneth with Thee in the unity of the Holy Spirit, God, forever and ever. Amen.
- Creator and Preserver of mankind, Giver of spiritual grace, Bestower of eternal salvation: send, O Lord, Thy blessing upon this ring, and may what it signifies in mystery be fulfilled in fact. Amen.

Methodist

Initially, Protestant Reformers were skeptical of the ring ceremony and hence omitted the blessing from their services. Luther has no words said over the ring, while early Calvinists and Puritans did not even allow a ring to be given. The Elizabethan Anglicans, on the other hand, made a clever compromise: Rather than blessing it, the groom placed the ring on the Bible before he put it on the bride's finger as a way of consecrating it to God.

Following Calvin, the United Methodist Church had also removed the ring from their weddings, but in 1864 they reintroduced the ancient custom.

The minister, taking the ring or rings, shall say:

The wedding ring is the outward and visible sign of an inward and spiritual grace, signifying to all the uniting of this man and woman in holy matrimony, through the Church of Jesus Christ our Lord.

Let us pray.

Bless, O Lord, the giving of these rings, that they who wear them may abide in Thy peace and continue in Thy favor; through Jesus Christ our Lord. Amen.

GIVING THE RING

What good is a ring if it is not worn? Next to the exchange of vows, the newlyweds' placement of rings on each other's fingers is the most tender part of the ceremony. These old formulas will add great charm, meaning, and even drama to this simple gesture.

Jewish

The Jewish rite retains the ancient custom of giving only the bride a wedding ring. According to Jewish law, the groom's proffering of an object and the bride's acceptance of it are essential to making the marriage valid. This act, called *kinyan,* is thought to be undermined when a mutual exchange of rings takes place instead.

After drinking the first cup (see above), the groom takes a ring of gold, shows it to the witnesses, and places it on the forefinger of her right hand (it can be removed later and worn on whatever finger the bride wants). He then says to her in Hebrew and English: "Behold, with this ring thou art wedded to me, according to the law of Moses and Israel."

Roman Catholic (Tridentine)

In this rite, the man's simple pledge of faith (troth) is enhanced by the Church's abundant prayers for the new couple.

The man puts the ring on the fourth finger of his wife's left hand, saying:

With this ring I thee wed, and I plight unto thee my troth.*

The priest then blesses them:

In the name of the Father, and of the Son, ✠ and of the Holy Spirit. Amen.

The priest then says several verses from the Psalms, with the servers, congregation, or choir responding:

P.   Confirm, O God, what Thou hast wrought in us.

R.   From Thy holy temple, which is in Jerusalem.

P.   Lord, have mercy.

R.   Christ, have mercy.

P.   Lord, have mercy.

The Our Father is said silently until . . .

P.   And lead us not into temptation.

R.   But deliver us from evil.

P.   Save Thy servants.

R.   Who hope in Thee, O my God.

P.   Send them help, O Lord, from the sanctuary.

R.   And defend them out of Sion.

P.   Be unto them, Lord, a tower of strength.

* In some places the following was used instead: "With this ring I thee wed; this gold and silver I thee give; with my body I thee worship; and with all my worldly goods I thee endow."

R.   From the face of the enemy.

P.   Lord, hear my prayer.

R.   And let my cry come before Thee.

P.   The Lord be with you.

R.   And with Thy spirit.

The priest then says:

Let us pray:

    Look with favor, O Lord, we beseech Thee, upon these Thy servants, and graciously assist Thine institutions by which Thou hast ordained the propagation of the human race: that they who are yoked together by Thy authorship may be protected by Thy help. Through Christ our Lord. Amen.

Anglican

The groom's eye-opening statement about worshiping his wife with his body sounds cheekier than it really is: centuries ago, "worship" simply meant "respect." This formula was used in medieval England long before it was taken up by the Church of England in 1549, but it somehow seems appropriate for the Elizabethan Age. No wonder Shakespeare was so colorful — he had a rich linguistic world from which to draw.

With this ring I thee wed; with my body I thee worship, and with all my worldly goods I thee endow. In the name of the Father and of the Son and of the Holy Ghost. Amen.

Then the man leaving the ring upon the fourth finger of the woman's left hand, the Minister shall say.

O eternal God, creator and preserver of all mankind, giver of all spiritual grace, the author of everlasting life: send thy blessing upon these thy servants, this man and this woman, whom we bless in thy name, that as Isaac and Rebecca (after bracelets and Jewels of gold given of the one to the other for tokens of their matrimony) lived faithfully together: So these persons may surely perform and keep the vow and covenant betwixt them made, whereof this ring, given and received, is a token and pledge. And may they ever remain in perfect love and peace together: And live according to thy laws: through Jesus Christ our Lord. Amen.

Then shall the Priest join their right hands together and say.

Those whom God hath joined together, let no man put asunder.

Episcopalian

The American liturgical architects kept these prayers essentially intact, except for shortening the groom's line to:

With this ring I thee wed, and with all my worldly goods I thee endow: in the name of the Father, and of the Son, and of the Holy Ghost. Amen.

For the Episcopalian (and later Anglican) changes to the concluding blessing, see p. 113.

Presbyterian

The Presbyterian church at the turn of the last century used this simple and elegant formula.

This ring I give thee, in token and pledge, of our constant faith and abiding love.

Methodist

This traditional declaration is similar to its Presbyterian cousin.

In token and pledge of our constant faith and abiding love, with this ring I thee wed, in the name of the Father, and of the Son, and of the Holy Spirit. Amen.

A common custom is to invoke the Blessed Trinity when putting the ring on the finger of one's spouse. The ring is placed first on the index finger with the words "In the name of the Father," then on the middle finger with the words, "and of the Son," and finally on the ring finger with, "and of the Holy Spirit. Amen." One medieval variation is: "N., with this ring I thee wed and take as my wife and my spouse; and I consent to it, in the name of the Father who created and remembers thee, and of the Son who redeems thee, and of the Holy Spirit who enlightens thee." Another option is to place the ring on the thumb when invoking the Father, on the index finger when invoking the Son, on the middle finger when invoking the Holy Spirit, and on the ring finger when saying, "Amen."

Tying the Knot

Though not necessarily prescribed by the rubrics, another common custom among many Roman Catholic, Protestant, and even several Byzantine churches was the wrapping of the priest's or minister's stole around the clasped hands of the couple and formally declaring them married. This simple gesture, which can be found in some non-Christian religions as well, generally takes place after the exchange of vows and has come to symbolize the new union of man and wife happily blessed by God and church (though it can also symbolize a newly betrothed couple; see p. 12). So important was this ceremony in the eyes of popular imagination that from it comes one of our colloquialisms for getting married: tying the knot.

The *Arrhae,* or Coins

Traditional Christian and Jewish marriages capture not only the sublime exhilaration of love, but the sober earthiness of practical matters. In Jewish services this is expressed in the *ketubah* (see Chapter IV), while in the Latin West it was customary to have the blessing of the *arrhae,* or earnest money. Earnest money is what is given in a bargain as a pledge of sincerity. In medieval weddings it represented the *dower,* the bride's portion of her new husband's estate which could not be taken away from her by his family in the event of his death. (Our referring to rich widows as "dowagers" comes from this arrangement.) Later, after the decline of landed gentry, the *arrhae* (or in Spanish, *arras*) came to signify the husband's obligation to work and provide for his wife and family. Money could even substitute for a wedding ring: A poor peasant couple would often use a coin with their names stamped on it and broken in two when a ring was too dear.

The Christian tradition of giving coins as a token of the earnest money goes back at least to the 400s and is still practiced today all over the world. The custom takes its precedent from the biblical stories of Isaac and Rebecca as well as Jacob and Rachel, where earnest money plays a prominent role in their courtships. Over the centuries the custom became highly stylized. In France, for example, the husband would give his wife thirteen *deniers,* a coin roughly equivalent to our dime. Thirteen was considered a lucky number because it was the sum of Christ and His twelve apostles, while the small value of the coins taught the newlyweds to hold temporal goods in low esteem. The coins would often have stamped on them images, such as two hearts on fire or two hands joined together, or inscriptions, such as "United Forever" or "One Faith from Two Hearts." They would be placed in a box (which could also have an inscription on it) and blessed during the service, imediately after the exchange of rings. Later the box would be placed under a glass beneath the hearth of the home, to protect the couple from misfortune and to remind them of fiscal responsibility.

This old French custom is by no means unique. Filipinos, for example, have an elaborate and meaningful *arrhae* tradition. Rather than having the groom give the coins to the bride, the priest empties loose coins into the groom's open hand, who then does the same to the bride. The bride, in turn, gives the coins back to the groom, who hands them off to an acolyte. The coins cascading from one hand to the next represent the bounty and grace of God poured forth on His children, as well as hope for prosperity and security. The handing of coins back and forth between husband and wife symbolizes not only the husband's obligations, but the wife's role as well, for in a traditional Filipino household it is she who manages the estate. (The flip-flopping of funds also reminds them that whatever one of them earns becomes the other's.) Given all the meaning attached to the *arrhae* ceremony, it is not surprising that Filipina bridal processions have a coin-bearer along with the more familiar ring-bearer.

Not all coin traditions, incidentally, are quite so codified. Some Scottish couples include a blessing of coins at their wedding, but they may have antique pieces which their parents or grandparents had used or recently minted commemorative coins. (Some have even used ordinary coins from their pockets.) In Spain, the groom simply gives the bride coins some time before the wedding so she can carry them with her in procession up the aisle, while in Hungary the groom gives the bride a bag of coins at the same time that the bride gives the groom (for reasons unclear to us) several handkerchiefs.

We have more to say about this symbolically rich custom in the Advice section of this chapter. In the meantime here are a few of the old blessings once said over the earnest money.

THE BLESSING OF COINS

The Rose of Jericho

The reference to the rose planted in Jericho comes from the book of Ecclesiasticus (Sirach), where Wisdom says that she is "exalted like a palm tree in Cades, and as a rose plant in Jericho" (24:18). The choice of Jericho is appropriate, since the name means "place of fragrance."

> Bless, O Lord, this earnest money, which today Thy servant N. puts into the hand of Thy handmaiden N., as Thou didst bless Abraham and Sarah, Isaac and Rebecca, Jacob and Rachel. Grant them the grace of Thy salvation, an abundance of things, and the constancy of work. May they flower as the rose planted in Jericho, and may they fear and adore our Lord Jesus Christ Thy Son, who liveth and reigneth with Thee, God the Father, in the unity of the Holy Spirit, God, forever and ever. Amen.

The Riches of Grace and Glory

This blessing is quick to subordinate the financial concerns of the couple to spiritual riches.

> Bless, O Lord, these coins, which we bless in Thy name, entreating Thine immense clemency: that whoever is endowed with them, may be divinely endowed with the riches of grace and glory — here, in eternity, and forever and ever. Amen.

The Bond of Love

This elaborate blessing begins with the biblical precedent of Isaac and Rebecca and ends with a series of entreaties to God.

> O Lord God Almighty, who didst desire to bind Isaac with Rebecca in the likeness of holy matrimony through the transmission of Thy servant Abraham's earnest money so that a multitude of children might spring forth by the offering of this gift: we beseech Thy might, that Thou, O Sanctifier, might approach the offering of this earnest money which Thy servant N. giveth to his beloved spouse N: and that Thou mayest kindly bless them along with their gifts. May they rejoice happily together as they are blessed by Thy protection and joined by the bond of love, and may they be forever delivered with Thy faithful ones. Through our Lord Jesus Christ Thy Son, who liveth and reigneth with Thee in the unity of the Holy Spirit, God, forever and ever. Amen.

THE ENDOWMENT OF COINS

The earnest money can be given at the same time as the ring. The following formulas encompass both the fiscal and the spiritual dimensions of the symbol quite nicely.

Feudal

N., with this ring I thee wed, with this silver I thee endow, and with my body I thee honor. In honor of God and of holy Lady Mary and of all the saints and of my lord N., etc.

Simple

With this ring I thee wed, with my body I thee honor, and with this dower I thee endow.

Apostolic

This endowment involves three coins instead of thirteen.

The groom takes two coins and says:

And with these two coins I thee endow in the name of the twelve Apostles.

He puts them in the hand of his bride. He then takes the last coin and, also putting it in her hand, says:

And with this third coin I thee endow in the name of Jesus Christ and of the whole Trinity.

Legal

The above endowment also added a rare feature in Christian weddings: a written contract.

The man takes the contract and says:

And with these pages here I confirm all, and I praise thy dowry, and I commend my goods to thee, that you may do good, for yourself and for me, and for the souls of our parents.

The woman then replies:

And I receive thee thus.

They then kiss each other as a sign of confirmation and faith.

Mexican

There are a number of coin blessings and declarations in use around the world today. We cannot include them all, but the following excerpt from the latest sacramentary of the Catholic Church in Mexico at least demonstrates how widespread and popular this custom is.

> *The man takes the coins and says:*
>
> Receive these coins; they are a pledge of the care I will take so that we will not lack what is necessary in our home.
>
> *The woman receives the coins and says:*
>
> I receive them as a sign of the care I will take so that our home will prosper.*

A Good Book

A marriage is meant to promote the deepest convictions of both couple and community, and so it is not surprising to find that some weddings emphasize the importance of Sacred Scripture in deed as well as in word. Filipino Protestants, for example, have a Bible-bearer process up the aisle along with the ring-bearer and, at an appropriate point in the ceremony, the minister blesses the holy book and declares it the couple's family Bible. Similarly, among Mexican Catholics there is an old custom of having a pair of sponsors *(padrinos)* present a *libro y rosario* (a prayer book or Bible and a rosary) to the bride after the vows are exchanged.

Presentation of Flowers to the Mother of God

A relatively recent custom among Roman Catholics is to present flowers to Mary, the Mother of God, after the communion rite. The custom,

* Translation by Timothy S. Matovina, "Marriage Celebrations in Mexican American Communities," *Liturgical Ministry* 5 (1996): 23.

which is most likely a century or two old, involves taking either the bridal bouquet or a specially designated bouquet of flowers over to a statue of Mary near the altar and laying it at her feet. The bride may do this by herself or she may be accompanied by the groom; in either case, some arrangement of "Ave Maria" is usually sung when this takes place, and it is not uncommon for the bride and groom to kneel briefly in private prayer once they reach the statue. The gift of flowers to the Blessed Virgin is meant to thank her for her prayers and to seek her intercession for a happy and holy marriage.

The Kiss

The kiss does not always appear in official church rubrics, but that does not make it insignificant. One of the images of a traditional wedding firmly etched in our minds is that of the new husband and wife sealing their vows in osculatory bliss as soon as the presider declares them married. (This can happen immediately after the exchange of vows or before the final procession down the aisle.) The kiss was actually an important legal element in pre-Christian Roman betrothals and weddings, though it came to designate quintessentially Christian realities. For example, even before the liturgical changes following the Second Vatican Council made the "Kiss of Peace" (known to most Catholics in the form of a handshake) a regular occurrence at Mass, there was a charming French custom from the seventeenth century that instructed the priest to impart the kiss of peace to the groom, who in turn imparted it to the bride. The form of this embrace in the traditional Roman rite bears only a vague resemblance to the wet kisses we generally associate with newlyweds, but the symbolism of the priest sharing God's peace with the married couple in an intimate, fraternal manner is unmistakable.

The Unity Candle?

To paraphrase Mark Antony, we come to bury the unity candle, not to praise it. The unity candle consists of three candles, one unlit and two lit. At some point in the service, the bride and groom each take a lit candle and simultaneously light the unlit candle, an action which symbolizes the two becoming one. The unity candle has gained a mild popularity in recent years, but it is, in our opinion, of dubious value. A commercially induced product rather than a custom with organic, religious origins, the unity candle came about in the 1960s or 1970s without great thought to its compatibility with Jewish or Christian symbolism. In Christian liturgies, for example, a lighted candle symbolizes Christ, the Light of the world. The bride and groom once processed up the aisle with lit candles, because as baptized Christians their souls were smaller lamps bearing witness to the divine Light. Similarly, two candles lit by special sponsors (the *ninong* and *ninang*) flank a Filipino wedding couple during the service, but the candles represent God's enlightenment and guidance in their married life, not them. Accordingly, a new marriage has never been symbolized by the lighting of a new candle for the simple reason that marriage is not the creation of a third soul or even the fusion of two souls: In wedlock, husband and wife become one flesh and hopefully one in spirit, but they do not metamorphose into one soul.

Another consideration is that the wedding ceremony already abounds in meaningful symbols of unity, such as the rings, the carecloth or crowning, and the kiss. Moreover, for many Christians at least, the supreme gesture of unity in the wedding service is the act of receiving Holy Communion together. The common cup in the Byzantine wedding, for instance, was actually introduced as a consolation for those couples from different religious backgrounds who could not receive communion together (couples planning for an interfaith wedding may wish to take note of this). Understandably then, the Vatican Congregation for Divine Worship as well as a number of Protestant churches have not permitted the use of the unity candle during the wedding ceremony.*

* In response to an inquiry about the use of the unity candle in the Catholic rite of marriage made by catholicliturgy.com, the Congregation stated on 29 December 1999 that any custom not approved by the National Conference of Bishops and "recognized" by the Vatican cannot be used in a Catholic wedding. The unity candle has never been approved by the U.S. Conference of Bishops, nor has it been granted a *recognitio* by the Holy See (see www.catholicliturgy.com/Index.cfm/FuseAction/LawText/Index/6/SubIndex/95/LawIndex/34).

Advice

There is something you may have noticed about these ceremonies: Many of them are remarkably similar to each other. This no doubt has a lot to do with a similar appreciation among traditional religions of the dignity and permanence of marriage. On the practical side, the commonality presents a unique opportunity for couples of different faiths to have a wedding which can incorporate elements from each tradition without having the end-product look contrived, mismatched, or awkward. As long as you do not add too many ceremonies at once, you will be able to enrich your service immensely. As we mentioned in the introduction, the beauty of traditional ceremonies is that they are almost guaranteed to succeed.

Those with no interdenominational concerns will, of course, also want to consider these customs. What follows is specific advice about each.

CHUPPAH

There are many options for obtaining a *chuppah*. Stores specializing in Jewish items often rent or sell them (consult your local yellow pages or the internet), and synagogues often have their own (consult your local rabbi). Some Jewish families keep their own *chuppah* as an heirloom to pass on to each new generation.

CARECLOTH

The Filipino wedding veil and cord *(yugal)* are inexpensive and relatively easy to find on the internet, as are Mexican *lazo* rosaries. A quick search on the internet will yield the URLs of several vendors. (Tip: in addition to using "Filipino," "wedding," "veil," "cord," or "yugal" as search words in various combinations, add "barong," a Filipino dress shirt usually sold at the same places as wedding paraphernalia. And for the rosaries, try "lasso" as well as "lazo" in conjunction with "wedding.") Do not forget, however, your local yellow pages.

European-style carecloths are too rare to be bought at this time, but they are easy enough to make. Michael's mother, for example, made a 4′ × 6′ carecloth out of white satin and sewed onto it a thick red curtain cord across its length (in accordance with the custom). And instead of choosing between the two different usages described above, Michael and Alexandra used both. First the carecloth was held above their heads while the Solemn Nuptial Blessing was prayed over them, and then it was draped over their shoulders from the end of the blessing until the next pause in the service (the Kiss of Peace). They also hope that this will start their own family tradition and will be used by their children and grandchildren. If, however, making your own carecloth is not a feasible option, we would recommend buying a couple's wedding veil from a Filipino store or website, since liturgically there is no significant difference between the two.

CROWNS

Whether you need to buy a pair of crowns for your Byzantine wedding depends on the custom of your church. In a Greek wedding, the best man, or *koumbaros*, traditionally buys the crowns, along with the candles held by the couple and a silver tray used in the service (again the internet will be a handy resource in finding religious stores that cater to Orthodox clients); after the wedding, husband and wife display their crowns in a *stephanothiki* (crown box) at home. On the other hand, Slavic parishes (Ukrainian, Russian, Belorussian, etc.) tend to have their own crowns for the couple to use, most likely because the grander, imperial crowns favored by some Slavs are considerably more expensive. Nevertheless, a Slavic couple may obtain their own gold crowns as a lasting keepsake for themselves or donate a set to their parish. This is not difficult to do, for these too may be purchased on the internet. Finally, couples may wish to consider having a good florist make a pair of natural garlands for the crowns, for many Byzantine Christians (Slavic and non-Slavic) prefer wreaths. As always, it is advisable to consult one's parish priest to learn the parameters of one's particular tradition.

Though bridal tiaras are also plentiful (check your local bridal shops and jewelry stores), one may be hard pressed to find Scandinavian wedding crowns in this country. Traditionally, it was the church that lent the crown to the bride (who wore it right through the reception), but we do not know which Scandinavian parishes in the U.S. have their own. Some clubs or organizations that preserve either Swedish or Norwegian or Finnish culture, however, have been known to possess their own crown, which they lend to members. At the very least they might be a good source of information or advice.

THE LOVING CUP

In Chapter VII we will discuss the purchase and use of loving cups for Western Christian receptions. Here, however, we will limit our remarks to Jewish and Byzantine cups.

One of the options Jewish couples can take advantage of is making one of the cups used in the ceremony a lasting keepsake. Silver or pewter *kiddush* cups are a longstanding tradition and can be easily found at Judaica shops or on the internet. These have the obvious advantage of being around later for special occasions such as anniversaries or religious feasts.

The glass which is broken, on the other hand, can either be one of the cups used during the ceremony (usually the first) or it can be a third glass already wrapped and ready for smashing. Either way, it does not have to be distinctive; any ordinary glass will do. Oftentimes friends or family like to give a glass as a gift in order to make a special contribution to the service. But regardless of what option you choose, it is important to have the glass carefully wrapped to prevent flying shards. A white napkin is the most common arrangement, but a special velvet pouch can also be made or purchased for the occasion.

Byzantine Christians, on the other hand, do not have to worry about obtaining a common cup. Like the chalice used for Holy Communion, the common cup used in the Divine Liturgy of St. John Chrysostom typically belongs to the church, which is why church goods stores tend to be the only suppliers. If you would like your own common cup, consult your parish priest to see if this is possible (in some places it is). If it is not, you may wish to consider donating a common cup to the parish. This is not only a gracious act of charity in itself, but it has the added advantage of providing something beautiful for your wedding and the weddings of others.

The Ring

As we mentioned above, the wedding ring was once given only to the bride because it originally signified her dower. Within the past generation or two, however, it has become common to have two rings. This arrangement in no way compromises the traditional spirit of your wedding. The blessings listed above can be easily made to refer to two rings, and the woman can simply repeat the man's words at the exchange.

Coins

The custom of giving coins, which is still found in several pockets of the world (no pun intended), makes sense especially when two wedding rings are being used. With two rings there is no longer the symbolism of a husband's obligation to care for his family (a psychologically important component for males, even in the age of two-income families), let alone the general virtue of fiscal responsibility. Before deciding how many or what kind of coins to use, determine first whether there are any precedents in your own ethnic or religious background. Christians in Mexico, the Philippines, Puerto Rico, Venezuela, and other nations influenced by Spain, for example, use thirteen gold or silver coins, usually commemorative pieces. These coins can be purchased from vendors or websites that cater to these markets, along with special coin boxes and pouches.

But the custom can also be easily modified to make it more multicultural or even personal by using coins from places that are dear to the hearts of the bride and groom. Couples could start with a subway token from the city in which they met and then gather the rest of the coins from ancestral lands: pesos from Mexico, pence from Ireland, etc. One couple we know, for example, followed the old French custom of using thirteen pre-Revolution *deniers,* while another used one French *denier* and twelve U.S. "Mercury head" dimes (which are inexpensive and more readily available). The first couple put their coins in a velvet bag, while the second couple put theirs in a tiny olive wood box from Bethlehem that now sits atop their mantle over the fireplace.

In terms of selecting a coin, we suggest something that does not have a high face value because the coins are supposed to remind you to hold temporal goods in low esteem. We also recommend choosing a kind of coin that was once in circulation but is no longer — hence our earlier reference to Irish pence rather than euros. A coin that was once in circulation is a *real* coin (as opposed to a collector's item from a private mint) and thus bespeaks the real obligations of the endowment. On the other hand, a coin no longer in circulation has been "set aside" from the profane and is thus more appropriate for use in a sacred liturgy. In America, one attractive option is the silver U.S. Mercury dime. Minted from 1916 until 1945 and featuring the bust of Lady Liberty in a winged cap (symbolizing freedom of thought), the dime is quite handsome and easily obtainable at your local coin shop or on the internet.

If the coins mentioned so far do not appeal to you, you may wish to invoke another ancient custom: the *medaille de mariage,* a special medallion commemorating the wedding with your names and the date of your wedding. Many people of Irish descent, for example, use the claddagh, the ancient Irish symbol of love, friendship, and loyalty, as a motif in their weddings. This image of two hands holding a crowned heart could be stamped on a few pennies and used instead of standard coins.

A BOOK

Those who are not Filipino or Mexican may still wish to consider the presentation of a Bible to the couple. Incorporating this custom into one's wedding service may also be particularly desirable for couples who belong to different Christian churches, as it would stress what they have in common.

VI. Blessings

God,
the best maker of all marriages,
Combine your hearts in one!

Shakespeare,
King Henry V.iii.387, 8

CONSENT IS THE ESSENCE of a valid marriage, which is why the vows are so important. Grace, on the other hand, is the essence of a holy and happy marriage, which is why nuptial blessings have been equally revered. Whether it be a priest, rabbi, or minister acting on behalf of the believing community or a father bestowing his benediction on the newlyweds, blessings collect the deepest wishes of couple and congregation and direct them to the Best Maker of all marriages. Little wonder that no traditional wedding has ever been without its abundant share of prayers and blessings. Fortunately for today's couple, this translates into a plethora of options. This chapter will present a number of classic blessings gleaned from the great tradition. Afterwards, as always, we will offer advice on making the right choices.

A Father's Blessing

Since the days of Abraham, a father's blessing has been a treasured boon. Traditionally, one of the most moving blessings a father could give to his children was the one he gave his daughter as she was about to leave his home forever. In former times this benediction would be bestowed at the threshold of the family house before the bride joined in a special procession to the church. Nowadays it can still be given at home or in the vestibule of the church or synagogue before the beginning of the ceremony. It can also be given, as is the case among Mexican families, to both bride and groom. Wherever and however you have it, we predict that the parents will be most honored by the request and the bride or groom most touched by the gesture.

JEWISH

The traditional Jewish blessing can be used to great effect by the father of the bride before the signing of the *ketubah*.

> Our sister, may you be the mother of thousands of myriads.
> May God make thee like Sarah, Rebecca, Rachel, and Leah.
> The Lord bless thee and keep thee.
> The Lord make His countenance to shine upon thee,
>   and be gracious unto thee.
> The Lord lift up His countenance upon thee, and grant thee peace.

CHRISTIAN

There is no standard paternal blessing in the Christian tradition. Any of the blessings in this book can be adapted for the purpose, or for that matter, something can be rendered straight from the heart. Below is one example taken from old France:

> Beloved daughter, receive the blessing from a father and mother
>   who love you more than their own life.

Always be a good wife and a good mother, and may God
protect you in the course of your years.

Solemn Nuptial Blessings

We define here as "solemn" whatever nuptial blessing constitutes a high
point for the liturgy. Almost every service, regardless of faith, has such a
moment.

ROMAN CATHOLIC (TRIDENTINE)

The Roman Solemn Nuptial Blessing is the grandmother of all Christian
marriage blessings: Written before the 500s, it not only became the oldest and most continuously used blessing in Christendom, but was the
starting point for a number of other prayers as well. The Roman blessing
was regarded as tremendously powerful. The bride and groom could receive it only once in their lives: If one of them were marrying again, he
or she had to do without it the second time around. Further, it could
only be given by a priest at the Nuptial Mass during certain times of the
year. These special restrictions no doubt served to heighten its aura —
so much so, in fact, that by the nineteenth century the clergy had to remind couples that it was not essential to make their marriage valid!

The delivery of this benediction is quite dramatic. Immediately after the "Our Father" the couple approaches the altar and kneels at its
bottom step. The carecloth may then be placed either on or over them
(see Chapter V). The priest, who in the traditional Mass has been facing
the same direction as the people, now turns to them, and with out-
stretched hands, says:

Let us pray.

Be favorable, O Lord, to our supplications, and generously assist Thine institutions for which Thou hast established the increase of mankind: that what is joined together by Thine author-
ship may be preserved by Thine aid. Through our Lord Jesus Christ

Thy Son, who liveth and reigneth with Thee in the unity of the Holy Spirit, God, forever and ever. Amen.

Let us pray.

O God, who by the power of Thy strength hast made all things out of nothing; who, having set in order the beginnings of the universe, didst fashion woman to be man's inseparable helpmate, made in the image of God, so that Thou might give to the female body a beginning from male flesh, teaching that what hath pleased Thee to institute from one may never be separated:

O God, who by so sublime a mystery hast consecrated conjugal union, that Thou might foreshadow in the covenant of marriage the sacrament of Christ and the Church:

O God, by whom woman is joined to man, and the fellowship, established from the first, is bestowed with that blessing which alone was taken away neither by the penalty of original sin nor by the sentence of the Flood:

Look with favor upon Thy handmaid here present, who, about to be joined in the partnership of marriage, seeks Thy defense and protection.

May it be for her a yoke of love and peace.

Faithful and chaste, may she be married in Christ.

May she ever remain an imitator of holy women. May she be dear to her husband, as Rachel; wise, as Rebecca; long-lived and faithful, as Sarah.

May that infamous author of deceit usurp nothing in her by his deeds.

May she ever remain tied to the Faith and to the commandments.

Joined to one spouse, may she avoid illicit contact.

May she protect any weakness of hers with the strength of discipline. May she be sober in appearance, venerable in modesty, well-instructed in heavenly doctrine.

May she be fruitful in offspring.

May she be found good and innocent, and may she come to the rest of the blessed and the kingdom of heaven.

Any may they both see their children's children, unto the third and fourth generation, and come to the old age which they desire. Through the same Lord Jesus Christ Thy Son, who liveth and reigneth with Thee in the unity of the Holy Spirit, God, forever and ever. Amen.*

BYZANTINE

In the nuptial liturgy celebrated by Orthodox Christians and Byzantine-rite Catholics, the most important blessing takes place *before* the couple is married, i.e., before the crowning ceremony. This is the longest and certainly the most "biblical" nuptial blessing in Christendom; in fact, one could use this magnificent prayer without any of the scriptural readings and still walk away fully illuminated by the Bible's various treatments of marriage. The two voices are those of Deacon and Priest.

D.   Of the Lord let us make entreaty.

P.   O God, who art spotless, and the Creator of the whole universe, who, through Thy loving-kindness, didst transform into a woman the rib of the first father, Adam, and didst bless them, and say: "Be fruitful and multiply and subdue the earth": and didst declare them both a harmonious unity, by means of the joining together: for, "Therefore shall a man leave his father and his mother, and shall cleave unto his wife, and they shall be one flesh": and, "Whom God hath joined together, let not man put asunder": Who didst bless Thy servant Abraham, and open Sarah's womb, and make him father of many nations: Who didst graciously give Isaac to Rebecca, and didst bless her offspring: Who didst unite Jacob to Rachel, and of him didst raise up the twelve Patriarchs: Who didst graciously give to them, as the fruit of parentage, Ephraim and Manasseh: Who didst accept Zacharias and Elizabeth, and raise up the Forerunner as their offspring: Who didst rear from the root of Jesse, according to the flesh, the Ever-virgin, and of her didst become flesh, and wast born for the salvation of mankind: who

* Note: The Solemn Nuptial Blessing was revised by the Catholic Church in 1969. For the latest version, see *The Rites of the Catholic Church.*

through Thy unspeakable free gift, and great goodness, wast present in Cana of Galilee, and didst bless the marriage there, that Thou mightest manifest that lawful wedlock is Thy will, and the parentage that arises from it:

Do Thou, O most holy sovereign Master, accept the entreaty of us Thy suppliants, and as Thou didst come there, come also here by Thine unseen presence. Bless this marriage, and give to these Thy servants, N. and N., a peaceful life, length of days, sobriety, mutual love in the bond of peace, a long-lived seed, grace upon their children, and the everlasting crown of glory. Count them worthy to see their children's children. Preserve their bed from adulterous snares: and give to them of the dew of heaven from above, and of the fatness of the earth. Fill their houses with corn and wine and oil and every good thing, that they may impart also to them who need, granting therewith to those also who are here present with us all petitions for safety.

For a God of mercy, compassion and loving-kindness art Thou, and the glory we ascribe to Thee, with thy Eternal Father, and Thy most holy and good and life-giving Spirit, now, and always, even for ever and ever. Amen.

D.   Of the Lord let us make entreaty.

P.   Blessed art Thou, Lord our God, the ministering Priest of the mystical and spotless marriage, and Law-giver of that which is corporeal, the Guardian of immortality and the good Dispenser of the things of this life:

Do Thou also, now, O Sovereign Master, who in the beginning didst fashion man and set him as king of the universe and say: "It is not good that a man should be alone upon the earth; I will make him a help meet from him; and He took one of his ribs and fashioned a woman, and when Adam saw her, he said, 'This is now bone of my bones and flesh of my flesh; she shall be called Woman, because she was taken out of her Man'; Therefore shall a man leave his father and his mother and shall cleave unto his own wife, and the two shall be one flesh": and "Whom God hath joined, let not man put asunder":

Do Thou also now, O Sovereign Master, Lord our God, send

down Thy heavenly grace upon these Thy servants, N. and N., and grant to this maiden to be obedient to her husband in all things, and that this Thy servant may be head of his wife, that they may live according to Thy will.

Bless them, O Lord our God, as Thou didst bless Abraham and Sarah. Bless them, O Lord our God, as Thou didst bless Isaac and Rebecca. Bless them, O Lord our God, as Thou didst bless Jacob and all the Patriarchs. Bless them, O Lord our God, as Thou didst bless Joseph and Asenath. Bless them, O Lord our God, as Thou didst bless Moses and Zipporah. Bless them, O Lord our God, as Thou didst bless Joachim and Anna. Bless them, O Lord our God, as thou didst bless Zacharias and Elizabeth. Effectually defend them, O Lord our God, as Thou didst effectually defend Noah in the ark. Effectually defend them, O Lord our God, as Thou didst effectually defend Jonas in the belly of the whale. Effectually defend them, O Lord our God, as Thou didst effectually defend the three holy children from the fire, by sending down on them dew from heaven: and may that grace come upon them which was with the blessed Helen when she found the precious Cross.

Remember them, O Lord our God, as Thou didst remember Enoch, and Joseph, and Elijah. Remember them, O Lord our God, as Thou didst remember the holy forty Martyrs, by sending down crowns upon them from heaven. Remember them, O Lord our God, and also the parents who reared them: for the prayers of parents establish the foundations of houses. Remember, O Lord our God, Thy servants, the bridal-attendants, who have assembled unto this feast.

Remember, O Lord our God, Thy servant this N. here present, and Thy handmaid this N. here present, and bless them. Grant them fruit of the womb, fair offspring, harmony of souls and bodies. Exalt them, like the cedars of Lebanon, like a fruitful vine. Bestow seed-corn upon them, that having all sufficiency, they may abound unto every work that is good and well-pleasing to Thee; and may they see their children's children like olive plants around their table. And being well-pleasing in Thy sight, may they shine as stars of heaven, in Thee our Lord: to whom is due all glory and power and honor and worship, now, and always, for ever and ever. Amen.

JEWISH

The Seven Benedictions *(sheva b'rachot)* seal and conclude a Jewish wedding. These seminal prayers, which locate the couple in the midst of God's historical romance with His chosen people and also provide a benediction for the second cup of wine, are the oldest in the Judeo-Christian tradition. They were possibly used at the wedding of Joseph and the Virgin Mary and at the wedding of Cana, and they have certainly been used since the second century A.D. The following is an English rendering of the original Hebrew that is still chanted or said at the wedding.

I   Blessed art Thou, O Lord our God, King of the universe, who createst the fruit of the vine.

II   Blessed art Thou, O Lord our God, King of the universe, who hast created every thing for Thy glory.

III   Blessed art Thou, O Lord our God, King of the universe, who hast formed man.

IV   Blessed art Thou, O Lord our God, King of the universe, who hast formed man after Thy image, in the image of the likeness of Thy form, to establish him an everlasting structure; blessed art Thou, O Lord, who formest man.

V   O cause Thou the barren one [Jerusalem] to be glad and rejoice at the gathering of her children unto her speedily amidst joy; blessed art Thou, O Lord, who causest Zion to rejoice in her children.

VI   O Lord, cause these loving friends to rejoice, as Thou once didst send joy unto Thy creatures, whom Thou hast formed in the garden of Eden of old; blessed art thou, O Lord, who causest the bridegroom and bride to rejoice.

VII   Blessed art Thou, O Lord our God, King of the universe, who hast created gladness and joy, bridegroom and bride, love and brotherhood, delight and pleasure, peace and friendship: speedily, O Lord our God, let there be heard in cities of Judah and in the streets of

Jerusalem the voice of mirth and voice of gladness, the voice of the bridegroom and the voice of the bride, the voice of the merriment of the bridegrooms at their nuptial feasts, and of youths from their musical entertainments; blessed art Thou, O Lord, who causest them to prosper. "O give thanks to the Lord, for He is good; for His mercy endureth for ever." May joys increase in Israel, and sighs flee away.

LUTHERAN

In terms of beauty, this succinct prayer is one of the highlights of Luther's marriage service:

O God, who hast created man and woman and hast ordained them for the married estate, hast blessed them also with fruits of the womb, and hast typified therein the sacramental union of thy dear one, the Lord Jesus Christ, and the church, His bride: We beseech Thy groundless goodness and mercy that Thou wouldst not permit this Thy creation, ordinance, and blessing to be disturbed or destroyed, but graciously preserve the same; through Jesus Christ our Lord. Amen.

ANGLICAN/EPISCOPALIAN

After the transfer of the ring (see Chapter IV), the 1559 Anglican service,* the 1790 Episcopalian service, and several other Protestant denominations have the following:

O eternal God, Creator and Preserver of mankind, Giver of all spiritual grace, the Author of everlasting life: Send Thy blessing upon these Thy servants, this man and this woman, whom we bless in Thy name; that, as Isaac and Rebecca lived faithfully together, so these persons may surely perform and keep the vow and covenant

* For the 1549 Anglican blessing, see p. 89.

betwixt them made (whereof this Ring given and received is a token and pledge), and may ever remain in perfect love and peace together, and live according to Thy laws, through Jesus Christ our Lord. Amen.

CALVINIST

In pristine prose, Calvin emphasizes the moral dimensions of marriage. The blessing was said immediately after the Gospel (see Chapter III).

P.   Let us pray from the heart to our Father:

All-powerful, All-good, and All-wise God, Thou who from the beginning hast foreseen that at no point is it good for man to be alone; Thou who hast created for man a help like unto himself and didst ordain that the two become one:

We pray to Thee to give Thy grace and bounty, and to send Thy Holy Spirit upon those whom it hath pleased Thee to call to the holy estate of matrimony. In true and firm faith, according to Thy good will, may they live in holiness, surmounting all evil affections. May they live purely, edifying others in all honesty and charity, giving them Thy blessing, as did Thy faithful servants Abraham, Isaac, and Jacob. Having holy offspring, may they praise and serve Thee, teaching them and nourishing them in Thy praise and glory and in service to one's neighbor, for the advancement and exaltation of Thy holy church. Grant this, Father of mercy, through our Lord Jesus Christ Thy beloved Son. Amen.

May Our Lord fill you with every grace, and may He give you to live together in happiness, holiness, and longevity.

Biblical Blessings

Virtually all of the blessings in this chapter borrow from the Bible and can hence be called "biblical." But what we mean here are those blessings that were inspired by a benediction explicitly given in Scripture.

Two sets stand out. The first, the Aaronic Blessings, are based on a blessing given by the high priest Aaron, Moses' brother. The second, the Tobian blessings, are based on two blessings given to the newly wed Tobias and Sara in the Book of Tobias (Tobit), found in the Catholic and Orthodox Old Testament.

AARONIC

We include Aaron's original blessing, followed by several traditional variations of it.

> The Lord bless you and keep you;
> The Lord shew his face to you, and have mercy on you;
> The Lord turn his countenance to you, and give you peace.

Numbers 6:24-26

> May God the Father bless you, may Jesus Christ keep you, may the Holy Spirit enlighten you; and may the Lord make His face to shine upon you and be merciful to you. May He turn His countenance upon you and grant you peace. May He fill you with every spiritual blessing for the remission of all your sins, that you may have eternal life and may live forever and ever. Amen.

Used throughout Medieval Europe

> May the Lord bless you and may Christ keep you;
> May the Lord shine His face upon you and grant you peace, and may Christ fill you with every spiritual blessing for the remission of sins, for eternal life, for ever and ever. Amen.

England, 800s

TOBIAN

By far the most popular scriptural inspiration for nuptial blessings — at least in the Roman Catholic and early Anglican traditions — is from the

Book of Tobias (Tobit), which tells the tale of Sara, a young maiden stalked by a menacing demon. Seven times she married, only to have each of her husbands killed by the demon on their wedding night. The curse is broken by her eighth husband, the virtuous Tobias, who — according to the Vulgate manuscript (Tob. 6:16-22; 8:4) — abstained from conjugal relations on their wedding night to demonstrate the purity of his love for her (as it turns out, the other seven husbands had only married her for lust). Tobias and Sara's continence became the inspiration for the so-called "Nights of Tobias," one to three days in which couples voluntarily refrained from consummating their marriage in a gesture of mutual respect and pious self-control. (The custom is still popular with Irish newlyweds who make the first leg of their honeymoon a brief pilgrimage to "St. Patrick's Purgatory," an important shrine in Lough Derg, Country Donegal.) Moreover, two blessings narrated in the Book of Tobias became the foundation for a number of cherished nuptial benedictions. The first blessing was given on the happy day by Sara's father, Raguel, and the second was given later in the story by his kinsman Gabelus. As before, we begin with the original blessings, followed by the later variations.

> The God of Abraham, and the God of Isaac, and the God of Jacob be with you. May He join you together, and fulfill His blessing in you. Amen.
>
> Raguel's blessing, Tobias 7:15

> The God of Israel bless thee, because thou art the son of a very good and just man, and that feareth God, and doth almsdeeds: And may a blessing come upon thy wife and upon your parents. And may you see your children and your children's children, unto the third and fourth generation: and may your seed be blessed by the God of Israel, who reigneth forever and ever.
>
> Gabelus' Blessing, Tobias 9:9-11

> The God of Abraham, the God of Isaac, the God of Jacob be with you in good times and in bad.
> May He join you in His enduring favor;
> May His blessing fill you, so that you may see your children's chil-

dren, and may your seed be blessed by the God of Israel who liveth and reigneth with our Lord Jesus Christ Thy Son in the unity of the Holy Spirit, God, forever and ever. Amen.

England, 1100s

Look down, O Lord, from Thy holy heaven upon this union; and as Thou sent Thy holy angel Raphael to Tobias and Sara the daughter of Raguel, so too deign to send Thy blessing, O Lord, upon these youths: that in Thy charity they may dwell, in Thy will they may stand, and in Thy love they may live and grow old and be multiplied unto length of days. Through our Lord Jesus Christ Thy Son, who liveth and reigneth with Thee in the unity of the Holy Spirit, God, forever and ever. Amen.

France, 1100s

Lord, look down from Thy holy heaven with Thy gentle angel Raphael upon this union, that they may be healthy and becoming and gentle; and pour forth Thy blessing upon them. Through our Lord Jesus Christ Thy Son, who liveth and reigneth with Thee in the unity of the Holy Spirit, God, forever and ever. Amen.

France, 1200s-1500s

Concluding Blessings

In addition to the main blessing said at some point during the service, many traditions add a second blessing at the end. We have included several of them here.

GERMANY, 1502

Stretch forth, O Lord, the right hand of Thy heavenly aid upon Thy faithful ones: that they may seek Thee with all their heart and may merit to attain what they worthily desire. Through our Lord Jesus

Christ Thy Son, who liveth and reigneth with Thee in the unity of the Holy Spirit, God, forever and ever. Amen.

GERMANY, 1521

Almighty, everlasting God, Thou who by Thy power created our first parents Adam and Eve, and by Thy blessing sanctified and joined them together in the fellowship of marriage: sanctify and bless the hearts and bodies of these two here present, and join them together in the fellowship and love of true delight. Through our Lord Jesus Christ Thy Son, who liveth and reigneth with Thee in the unity of the Holy Spirit, God, forever and ever. Amen.

ENGLAND, 800S

Almighty God, make Thy providence accompany this pious love, so that those whom Thou dost join in lawful fellowship, Thou mightest keep in long-lived peace. Through our Lord Jesus Christ Thy Son, who liveth and reigneth with Thee in the unity of the Holy Spirit, God, forever and ever. Amen.

ENGLAND, 1100S

Look favorably, O Lord, upon Thy servant and upon Thy hand-maiden: that they may receive Thy heavenly blessing in Thy name, and live to see their children's children unto the third and fourth generation. May they always persevere in Thy faith, and may they reach the heavenly kingdom. Through our Lord Jesus Christ Thy Son, who liveth and reigneth with Thee in the unity of the Holy Spirit, God, forever and ever. Amen.

FRANCE, 1500S

May the Lord bless you with every spiritual blessing;
May He make you worthy in His sight;
May the riches of His glory abound in you, and may He teach you
in the word of truth: that you may merit to be pleasing to Him in
body and in mind. Amen.

SPAIN, 800S

Note the beautiful sentiments of these next two prayers, the first from
Spain and the second from Germany:

May the almighty Lord bless you by the words of our mouth, and
may He join your hearts by a perpetual bond of sincere love.

May you blossom from the abundance of things at hand.

May you be fruitful with children.

May you rejoice forever with friends.

May the Lord grant your enduring gifts, times spent happily
with parents, and above all, eternal joy.

Through Him who possesses the name One-and-Three and is
glorified, God forever and ever. Amen.

GERMANY, 1502 (2)

O God, who in the beginning of the blossoming world blessed its
numerous offspring, look favorably on our prayers and pour the aid
of Thy blessing upon Thy servant and Thy handmaiden: that they
be joined in conjugal fellowship, equal affection, similar minds, and
mutual holiness. Through our Lord Jesus Christ Thy Son, who
liveth and reigneth with Thee in the unity of the Holy Spirit, God,
forever and ever. Amen.

Tridentine

This concluding blessing, which combines both of the Tobian blessings, is given immediately before the final dismissal in the extraordinary form of the Roman rite.

> May the God of Abraham, the God of Isaac, and God of Jacob be with you, and may He fulfill His blessing in you, so that you may see your children's children unto the third and fourth generation. And hereafter, may you have eternal life without end, by the help of our Lord Jesus Christ, who liveth and reigneth with the Father in the unity of the Holy Spirit, God, forever and ever. Amen.

Byzantine

This prayer in the Byzantine liturgy is said after the Circling Procession (see Chapter V):

> O Lord our God, who in the ministry of salvation didst vouchsafe to render marriage honorable by Thy presence at Cana of Galilee: do Thou also, now, effectually defend in peace and harmony, Thy servants, N. and N., whom Thou hast been pleased to be joined to one another. Render their marriage honorable: Keep their bed wholly undefiled: Be pleased that their joining shall abide wholly unblemished, and count them worthy to arrive at a fruitful old age, doing Thy commandments with a pure heart.
>
> For Thou, O our God, art a God to have mercy and to save, and to Thee we ascribe the glory, with Thy Eternal Father, and Thy most holy, good and life-giving Spirit, now, and always, even for ever and ever. Amen.

The classic Episcopalian service ended with this blessing:

> God the Father, God the Son, God the Holy Ghost, bless, preserve, and keep you; The Lord mercifully with His favour look upon you, and fill you with all spiritual benediction and grace; that ye may so live together in this life, that in the world to come ye may have life everlasting. Amen.

The 1559 Anglican service goes on to add the following:

Then the Ministers, or Clerks, going to the Lord's table, shall say, or sing this Psalm following.

Beati omnes. cxxviii
[Psalm 128: "Blessed are all . . ."]

Or else this Psalm following.

Deus misereatur nostri. lxvii
[Psalm 67: "May our God have mercy . . ."]

Glory be to the Father and to the Son and to the Holy Ghost.
As it was in the beginning, is now, and ever shall be, world without end. Amen.

The Psalm ended, and the man and the woman kneeling afore the Lord's table: the Priest standing at the table, and turning his face toward them, shall say:

	Lord have mercy upon us.
Answer.	Christ have mercy upon us.
Minister.	Lord have mercy upon us.

	Our Father, which art, &c. And lead us not into temptation.
Answer.	But deliver us from evil. Amen.

Minister.	O Lord save Thy servant and Thy handmaid.
Answer.	Which put their trust in Thee.

Minister.	O Lord send them help from Thy holy place.
Answer.	And evermore defend them.
Minister.	Be unto them a tower of strength.
Answer.	From the face of their enemy.
Minister.	O Lord hear our prayer.
Answer.	And let our cry come unto Thee.
Minister.	O God of Abraham, God of Isaac, God of Jacob, bless these Thy servants, and sow the seed of eternal life in their minds, that whatsoever in Thy holy word they shall profitably learn, they may in deed fulfil the same. Look, O Lord, mercifully upon them from heaven, and bless them. And as Thou didst send Thy blessing upon Abraham and Sara, to their great comfort: so vouchsafe to send Thy blessing upon these Thy servants, that they obeying thy will, and always being in safety under Thy protection, may abide in Thy love unto their lives' end, through Jesus Christ our Lord. Amen.

This prayer next following shall be omitted where the woman is past child-birth.

O merciful Lord and heavenly Father, by whose gracious gift mankind is increased, we beseech thee, assist with Thy blessing these two persons, that they may both be fruitful in procreation of children, and also live together so long in godly love and honesty, that they may see their children's children unto the third and fourth generation, unto Thy praise and honour: through Jesus Christ our Lord. Amen.

O God, which by Thy mighty power has made all things of nought; which also after other things set in order, didst appoint that out of man (created after Thine own image and similitude) woman should take her beginning, and knitting them together, didst teach that it should never be lawful to put asunder those whom Thou by matrimony hadst made one: O God, which hast consecrated the state of matrimony to such an excellent mystery, that in it is signified and represented the spiritual marriage and unity betwixt Christ and His Church; Look mercifully upon these Thy servants, that both this man may love his wife, according to Thy word (as Christ did love His spouse the Church, who gave Himself for it, loving and cherishing it, even as His own flesh), and also that this woman may be loving and amiable to her husband as Rachel, wise as Rebecca, faithful and obedient as Sara, and in all quietness, sobriety, and peace, be a follower of holy and godly matrons. O Lord, bless them both, and grant them to inherit Thy everlasting kingdom, through Jesus Christ our Lord. Amen.

Then shall the Priest say,

Almighty God, which at the beginning did create our first parents, Adam and Eve, and did sanctify and join them together in marriage, pour upon you the riches of His grace, sanctify and bless you, that ye may please Him both in body and soul, and live together in holy love unto your lives' end. Amen.

Consummation Blessings

These blessings were used for the blessing of the couple on their marriage bed (see Chapter VII), but we have included them here because they can easily be used in the service itself.

EASTERN FRANCE, 1513

May the blessing which the Lord poured forth upon Isaac
    come upon you;
May the blessing which Isaac amply gave to Jacob come unto you;
May the blessing which Jacob directed to his sons be extended,
    through God's gift, to you;
May the blessing which Moses bore upon the children of Israel
    be shared, through Christ's favor, in your hearts;
And may the blessing which our Lord Jesus Christ, the Redeemer

of all, gave to His disciples abundantly reach your bodies
and souls.

Through the same our Lord Jesus Christ Thy Son, who liveth
and reigneth with Thee in the unity of the Holy Spirit, God,
forever and ever. Amen.

IRELAND/SPAIN, 800S

This beautiful blessing has two pedigrees because it was written by Irish
missionaries and used in Spain.

> Let us pray, beloved brethren, to God, who deigned to spread the
> gifts of His blessing in order to increase the offspring of mankind:
> that He may watch over these His servants, N. and N., whom He
> hath chosen for the embrace of marriage. May He grant unto them
> gentle affection, similar minds, conduct bound in mutual love. If He
> should so wish, may they have children, whom He bestows as a
> gift. And thus may His blessing follow: that these His servants, N.
> and N., may zealously serve in the humility of one and the same
> heart Him whom they do not doubt to be their Creator. Amen.
>
> We pray, O holy Lord, almighty Father, everliving God, for Thy
> servants, N. and N., whom Thou hast bid to come to the grace of
> marriage, and who have longed for Thy blessing through our voice
> and prayers. Grant them, O Lord, the faithful fellowship of charity.
> May they put on the charity of Sarah, the wisdom of Rebecca, the
> love of Rachel, and the grace of Susannah. May Thy hand descend
> upon Thy servants, N. and N., as the dew of rain descends upon the
> face of the earth. May they quietly sense Thy Holy Spirit, and may
> they attain everlasting joy. Through our Lord Jesus Christ Thy Son,
> who liveth and reigneth with Thee in the unity of the Holy Spirit,
> God, forever and ever. Amen.

This is perhaps the second-oldest marriage prayer we have in Western Christianity. Note the tasteful allusions to the wedding night.

> Holy Lord, almighty Father, everliving God, with whom is Christ our Mediator, we humbly entreat Thee again with prayers on behalf of Thy servants whom Thou hast deigned to cherish with this union. May they be worthy to receive Thy blessings, that they may be fruitful with children by what follows. Deign to strengthen their marriage, as Thou hast done with many. May all snares of the enemy be driven far away from them. And may they, O Lord, who by Thy providence will be joined together in purity, imitate in this marriage the holiness of the Fathers. Through our Lord Jesus Christ Thy Son, who liveth and reigneth with Thee in the unity of the Holy Spirit, God, forever and ever. Amen.

Advice

When it comes to blessings, we advise aiming high. This is, after all, your wedding and your life, and there is nothing wrong in trying to obtain as many favors from above as possible. (It also does not hurt to have such beautiful sentiments articulated at your service for the edification and delight of yourselves and your guests.) We have confidence in the blessings presented in this chapter. Like the medieval vows, we were happy to find such a variety of well-written and meaningful blessings hidden in old and dusty books, and we have no hesitation in recommending them for your service. We are also of the opinion that, with proper prudence, a blessing can be used other than it was originally intended. A conclusion blessing, for example, could be put at a different point in the service. To help you with your particular choices, we offer the following guidelines:

First, make sure you know what the blessing is saying. Catholics, for example, might find the Calvinist blessing objectionable or vice versa.

Second, strive for harmony. Avoid needless redundancy and try to find blessings that are complementary (thematically, biblically, etc.).

Third, choose no more than three blessings for the service. Depending on what kind of ceremony you have, a blessing at the beginning, middle, and end is sufficient. Blessings immediately before or after the exchange of vows are especially appropriate. Consult your pastor to determine how many blessings are customary and which ones you can choose for yourself.

Blessings can also have a use outside of the service. A blessing of which you are fond can appear on the front of your program in calligraphy, or a number of lines from various blessings can be brought together to form a memorable wedding toast.

VII. Postnuptials

Proceed, proceed:
  we will begin these rites,
As we do trust
  they'll end in true delights.

Shakespeare,
As You Like It V.iv.204-5

I T IS NO COINCIDENCE that in many languages the word for "wedding" is in the plural rather than the singular. This is a small reminder that the celebration of a marriage consists of several stages. We move now to the last of them. Your sacred joining was, appropriately enough, expressed in a tone of bridled glee and poignant petition. And your celebration of that joining is now, appropriately enough, to be expressed in greater exuberance, an explosion of joy. Postnuptial customs — or more accurately, penultimate and ultimate nuptial customs — capture the true delights which await the newly married couple.

We proceed chronologically, from the first things that follow the service to the customs that can happen as many as eight days later. And we will close, as is *our* custom, with general suggestions.

Before the Reception: *Yichud*

Yichud is a space of ten minutes or so in the Jewish tradition for the newly married couple to spend with each other in complete privacy. Once the time for physical consummation and now the time for emotional consummation, *yichud* offers the bride and groom a moment of calm before the excitement of the festivities that follow. The *heder yichud*, or room in which this takes place, is kept a strict secret.

At the Reception

We mentioned in the general introduction that weddings are a wonderful time to discover family traditions. This is especially true regarding the reception, where most family nuptial customs naturally congregate. Ask your parents or relatives if there is anything which they or their parents had done at their weddings. Perhaps even your brothers or sisters began a tradition which you would like to continue. Small customs from one's past go a long way in making a celebration that much more memorable — for you and for your guests.

Of course, small customs from one's past (more broadly understood) also go a long way. The following is a sampling of traditional wedding feast customs.

THE LOVING CUP

As we mentioned in Chapter V, the loving cup is traditionally reserved in Western Christianity for the wedding feast or reception. This was considered a good time to have the cup because of its connection to Christ's miracle of changing water into wine at the wedding feast of Cana. Over time different nationalities developed charming variations of the loving-cup tradition. The Scottish and the Irish, for example, are known to use a loving cup called a *quaich,* which comes from the Gaelic word for "cup." The *quaich* is a small silver or pewter bowl with two extended side handles and, originally, a double glass bottom in which a lock of the bride's hair would be kept. The *quaich* has had many social uses, but it has been a favorite at weddings ever since King James VI of Scotland gave one to his bride Anne of Norway as a wedding gift in 1589. Similarly, the French were traditionally fond of a double-handed goblet appropriately called a *coupe de mariage* (marriage cup). Elegant and often ornate, it could serve as a family heirloom after it served its purpose at the reception.

One particularly interesting loving cup is the "Nuremberg Bridal Beaker" from southern Germany. The legend is that a lowly goldsmith fell in love with a noble maiden named Kunigunde. Her father, wishing to keep them apart, told the smith that he could marry her only if he could make a cup from which two people could drink at the same time without spilling a drop. The goldsmith's solution was to fashion a pewter woman with a hollow dress holding a swiveling cup. The news of the goldsmith's success quickly spread throughout all of Bavaria, where the Bridal Beaker has been used ever since.

We are including a good example of a cup blessing from medieval England; the cup blessings in Chapter V, of course, are also appropriate.

> Bless, O Lord, this drink and this cup. And as Thou didst bless the six stone vases in Cana of Galilee and made wine out of water, so too deign to bless and sanctify this drink and this cup with Thy perpetual blessing: that whoever tastes of it may come to prosperity in the present age and be worthy of eternal joy in the next. Who livest and reignest with God the Father in the unity of the Holy Spirit, God, forever and ever. Amen.

For the Jewish use of the loving cup during the reception, see the section below on grace after meals.

THE BLESSING OF THE BREAD

Before wedding cakes, there was wedding bread. In its most simple form, the bride and groom would have a single loaf blessed after the Mass, and each would take a piece; in its more elaborate variations (which we will discuss in the advice section), tasty national and ethnic breads would have a prominent place in the wedding fare. The following is a typical medieval blessing.

> Bless, O Lord, this bread as Thou didst bless the five loaves in the desert: that all tasting it may obtain health in body and soul. Who livest and reignest with God the Father in the unity of the Holy Spirit, God, forever and ever. Amen.

A similar custom is also found in Judaism. The wedding feast traditionally begins with the blessing of *challah,* the rich, braided white bread used on the Sabbath and other holy days. The blessing can be said by anyone.

> Blessed art Thou, Lord God, King of the Universe, who bringest forth bread from the earth.

THE TOAST

The custom of toasting has no religious significance per se, but it has become so ingrained in our idea of what a nuptial celebration involves that it would be remiss of us to overlook it. Accordingly, we include this special section on toasts to help you craft or deliver the perfect encomium to the bride and groom.

If you are short on ideas for something to say, we first recommend perusing the blessings included in this book. With a slight alteration of words, virtually any of these can be made into a touching and appropriate toast. If, however, the service was plentiful in thoughts sublime, perhaps something more light or humorous would make a nice contrast. Poetry is also an excellent source for these kinds of fond feelings and good wishes. The following is a selection of some of our favorite nuptial poems and toasts.

To the Bride from the Groom

> Drink to me only with thine eyes,
> And I will pledge with mine;

Or leave a kiss within the cup
And I'll not look for wine.
The thirst that from the soul doth rise
Doth ask a drink divine;
But, might I of love's nectar sip,
I would not change for thine.

Ben Jonson

Come with me and be my love,
And we will all the pleasures prove,
That valleys, groves, or hills or fields
Or woods or sleepy mountains yield.

Christopher Marlowe

To thee, my love, I drink the cup,
Then leave my soul therein:
That when thy dear mouth drinks to me
I'll enter heaven without sin.

W. E. P. French, modified

To see her is to love her,
And love but her for ever;
For Nature made her what she is,
And ne'er made such another.

Scottish Toast

Fair is my dove, my loved one,
None with her can compare:
Yea, comely as Jerusalem,
Like unto Tirzah fair.

White lilies and red roses
There blossom on one stem:
Her lips of crimson berries
Tempt mine to gather them.

Postnuptials   131

Her beauty shames the day-star,
And makes the darkness light;
Day in her radiant presence
Grows seven times more bright.

This is a lonely lover!
Come, fair one, to his side,
That happy be together
The bridegroom and the bride!

"The Marriage Song,"
by Judah Halevi, abridged

To the Groom from His Father

Jewish

My son, on this thy wedding day rejoice,
To song of mirth attune thy heart and voice.
Take thou the graceful doe, the royal bride,
With her thy joy and happiness divide.
A comely form, my darling son, is thine;
Corrupt it not, for 'tis a gift divine.

Three crowns there are, and these the world may love;
A blameless name is more, all crowns above.
Humbly pray God may crown thee with His light,
To live 'mid men, with heart, with soul, with might.
Rejoice with her, thy graceful tender dove;
God bless you twain, with love as angels love.

from the "Silver Bowl," by Josephy Ezobi

Christian

St. John tells how, at Cana's wedding-feast,
The water-pots poured wine in such amount
That by his sober count
There were a hundred gallons at the least.

It made no earthly sense, unless to show
How whatsoever love elects to bless
Brims to a sweet excess
That can without depletion overflow.

Which is to say that what love sees is true;
That the world's fullness is not made but found.
Life hungers to abound
And pour its plenty out for such as you.

Now, if your loves will lend an ear to mine,
I toast you both, good son and dear new daughter,
May you not lack for water,
And may that water smack of Cana's wine.

Richard Wilbur, "A Wedding Toast"

To the Bride and Groom

Blessed are the vows of wedded life,
When they from righteous lips proceed,
When, love ennobling man and wife,
Time hallows that which God decreed.

from "Blest Is the Bond" by Penina Moise

May the hinges of friendship never rust
nor the wings of love lose a feather.

Scottish Toast

May you be poor in misfortune, rich in blessings,
Slow to make enemies, quick to make friends.
But rich or poor, quick or slow,
May you know nothing but happiness
From this day forward.

Irish Toast

The bride was one, and one was the groom,
Yet, now that the sum is done,
We drink to a pair in paradox —
The two that are only one.

W. E. P. French

May the road rise up to meet you;
May the wind be always at your back;
May the sun shine warm upon your face
And the rain fall soft upon your fields.
Until we meet again
May God hold you in the hollow of His hand.

Irish Toast

May their joys be as deep as the ocean,
Their sorrows as light as its foam;
May the sunlight of love ever brighten
Their lives and shine into their home.

W. E. P. French

The world was sad, the garden wild,
And man, the hermit, sighed — till woman smiled.

Thomas Campbell

Though the following poem was meant to be used in its entirety, we
think that one or two of its stanzas would also be sufficient. Another alternative would be to have a round of toast-givers, preferably with a flare
for the theatrical, each one delivering a stanza.

Here's to the health of the happy pair,
May good luck meet them everywhere,
And may each day of wedded bliss
Be always just as sweet as this!

Let us drink to the health of the bride,
Let us drink to the health of the groom,

Let us drink to the Parson who tied
And to every guest in the room!

Here's to the union which we had sought,
And this union just begun,
"Two souls with but a single thought —
Two hearts that beat as one!"

These two, now standing hand in hand,
Remind us of our native land;
For when today they linked their fates,
They entered the united states!

W. E. P. French

JEWISH GRACE AFTER THE MEAL

This beautiful prayer, called the *birkat hamazon,* concludes a traditional Jewish wedding feast. The designated leader takes a cup of wine, and praying over it, says:

> O Lord, banish sorrow and wrath from us, and then even the dumb will exult in song. Lead us in the paths of righteousness, and deign to accept the blessing of the sons of Jerusalem.
>
> With the permission of our sages and teachers, and with yours, gentlemen, we will praise our God, in whose abode dwells joy, and of whose gifts we have eaten.

All   Blessed be our God, in whose abode dwells joy, and of whose gifts we have eaten.

> *The leader now takes a second cup and recites the* sheva b'rachot *from the service (see Chapter VI), omitting the initial blessing. Then the leader takes the first cup and recites the initial blessing. At this point the wine from both cups is poured into a third cup from which the bride and groom drink.*

"Jumping the broom" is an ancient wedding ritual once found among the Celts and other tribes. It is associated especially, however, with the African-American antebellum South. Since slaves in Protestant-dominated states were legally prohibited from marrying, they invented their own custom to ratify the permanence of their love. Putting a broom on the floor, they held hands and jumped over it together. The symbolism was simple but beautiful: The broom represented hearth and home, while the jump signified the transition to domestic union. The broom was also ideal because it was not an object likely to arouse slaveholder suspicion.

The past few decades have witnessed a strong renewal of this custom among African-Americans eager to embrace or preserve their identity. Today jumping the broom is usually conducted at the reception after the official service. A special broom is purchased or made for this occasion, and afterwards it is proudly displayed in the new couple's home as an heirloom. There are even presiders who can be hired for the reception to explain the history and meaning of the ritual.

After the Reception: Consummation Rites

Just as the few words of the wedding vow alter the whole course of one's life, no less is the conjugal act a defining moment. As Colette writes in *Noces,* "The day after that wedding night I found that a distance of a thousand miles, abyss and discovery and irremediable metamorphosis, separated me from the day before." Understandably, then, ceremony has always surrounded the bridal chamber on the wedding night. Decorating the marriage-bed with flowers and the Hymen Torch was *de rigueur* in ancient Greece, while the ritual undressing of the bride by her bridesmaids was a Christian custom (probably borrowed from the Romans) that lasted from the 300s until the turn of the last century. Judaism, too, has an elaborate code surrounding this night, as the Hebrew Bible amply attests.

There were also blessings of the marriage bed. Inspired by the "undefiled bridal-bed" mentioned in the letter to the Hebrews (13:4), these were prayers said by the priest over the couple as they sat upon their bed. Sometimes the parents of the newlyweds and other kin were in attendance. The blessings were followed by sprinkling the couple and the bed with holy water.

No doubt in today's world this custom would raise a few eyebrows. But for the ancient Christians, consummating the marriage was something sacred because it completed, in a sense, the sacrament of matrimony. And, of course, if an act is sacred there should be a blessing to go with it. Blessings of the marriage bed, therefore, not only guarded against the maladies which can plague the bedroom but affirmed the goodness and naturalness of this nuptial activity. And the ceremony still survives in interesting ways. Not only is it still officially listed in the liturgical manuals of several churches (e.g., the Catholic Church in Scotland), but in places like the Czech Republic there is an old custom of placing an infant on the couple's bed before the wedding to ensure a union blessed with little ones.

Here are a few of these blessings once prayed throughout Europe.

Bless, O Lord, this bed and all those upon it, that they may be filled with holiness and chastity and tenderness. Through our Lord Jesus Christ Thy Son, who liveth and reigneth with Thee in the unity of the Holy Spirit, God, forever and ever. Amen.

England, 800s

Look down upon Thy servants and upon Thy works, O Lord, and guide Thy children with Thy blessings.

Let us pray.

O Lord, in the fullness of whose blessing they stand who receive a blessing by the invocation of Thy name, bless this marriage-bed, prepared for honorable nuptials: that no curse of evil may touch it, but conjugal purity alone possess it, and that Thy mercy may be sufficiently present in its worthy and joyful use. Amen.

Ireland/Spain, 800s-1100s

Lord, Thou who dost never sleep, bless this bedchamber. And Thou who didst guard Thy people Israel, guard Thy servants resting here upon this bed from all the nightmares and manipulations of demons. Awake may they meditate on Thy precepts; asleep may they sense Thy presence. Through our Lord Jesus Christ Thy Son, who liveth and reigneth with Thee in the unity of the Holy Spirit, God, forever and ever. Amen.

Paris, 1481

Bless, O Lord, this marriage-bed and these Thy married servants: that in Thy peace they may stand, in Thy will they may remain, and in Thy love they may live and grow old and be multiplied unto length of days. Through our Lord Jesus Christ Thy Son, who liveth and reigneth with Thee in the unity of the Holy Spirit, God, forever and ever. Amen.

Paris, 1839

Not surprisingly, the story of Tobias and Sara inspired prayers for the wedding night as well as for the service. This English prayer from the 800s is one example:

Bless, O Lord, these youths, and as Thou didst bless Tobias and Sara, the daughter of Raguel: that in Thy name they may live and grow old and be multiplied unto length of days. Through our Lord Jesus Christ Thy Son, who liveth and reigneth with Thee in the unity of the Holy Spirit, God, forever and ever. Amen.

Note: For more consummation blessings, see Chapter VI, p. 123.

The Day After: Introducing the Newlyweds

In researching this book we were surprised to discover many different "introduction" customs for the bride and groom. These were generally informal rituals performed the day after the wedding night which introduced them back into church or society with their newfound identities.

More conventional ideas, such as a brunch with a small set of family and friends or a reception with one's parishioners, can keep alive the spirit of this tradition. The top layer of your wedding cake can be saved from the previous day and used for this event. A thoughtful relative or friend could even plan it for you, since it might be too much to take on the responsibility by yourself. (All of this is assuming, of course, that you are not impeded by a quick honeymoon departure.) For an older and more formal example, we have included here a medieval introduction rite for use in a church.

P.   Save, O Lord, this new bride;
R.   Who hopeth in Thee, my God.

P.   O Lord, hear my prayer:
R.   And let my cry come before Thee.

P.   The Lord be with you.
R.   And with thy spirit.

P.   Let us pray.
    Be present, we beseech Thee, almighty and merciful God, that this newly married woman, purified and cleansed in mind as well as in body, may serve Thee on earth and be numbered among Thy saints and chosen ones in heaven. Through our Lord Jesus Christ Thy Son, who liveth and reigneth with Thee in the unity of the Holy Spirit, God, forever and ever. Amen.

    Let us pray.
    Deign, O Lord, to bless and sanctify this newly married man and all those present here with Thy heavenly blessing. In the name of the Father and of the Son and of the Holy Spirit. Amen.

The Sunday After: Bride's Sunday and Kirkin'

Some of the more distinctive "introduction" customs are found among the Irish and Scottish. Be it called "Bride's Sunday" or "Kirkin'," the formal return of the married couple to their parish church on the Sunday following their wedding was reserved as a special event.

The Irish tradition of Bride's Sunday was a simple but meaningful affair. On the first Sunday following the wedding, the guests would escort the couple to Mass, usually leading the way. After Mass was over, all would adjourn to one of the bridesmaid's homes for tea and dinner.

The Scottish custom of Kirkin', on the other hand, was far more elaborate. Before the Sunday worship would begin, the bride would process to the church, accompanied by two young men; following her would be the groom, accompanied by two young maidens. At the church door the young men and maidens would step aside, and the bride and groom would enter together. The others followed, each side by side. At a pew specially reserved for them, the wedding group would sit in the following order: bride, maiden, young man, maiden, young man, and, closest to the aisle, groom. Sometimes a staff decorated with blue ribbons would be held by one of the young men during both the procession and the whole service. After the service, the groom would take one of the ribbons and wear it on his right arm for the rest of the day (before white bridal gowns became the norm, blue — the traditional color of purity — was worn; hence the lasting importance of wearing "something blue").

These customs would obviously be difficult to transpose into the contemporary context, but they do again remind us of the communal nature of marriage, particularly that of the religious community. Again, modern equivalents could easily be devised, such as a brunch held after the service (an especially good idea when there are still out-of-town guests in the area). And who knows, a groom of Scottish descent might just want to show up wearing a blue ribbon on his arm.

Eight Days After: The Dismissal of the Crowns

On the eighth day following the wedding, it was customary for Byzantine newlyweds to formally "dismiss" their crowns. After Holy Communion but before the final dismissal, the couple comes forward. The crowns are again set on their heads, and the priest says:

> O Lord our God, who hast blessed the bridal wreath of the year, and hast delivered to us that the present crowns should be set

upon those who are joining themselves to one another by the law of marriage, and dost allot this to them as a reward of sobriety, because chaste they were joined together in marriage which has been by Thee made lawful: do Thou also, at the putting away of the present crowns, bless those that have been joined to one another, and effectually preserve their union unbroken; so that they may give thanks through all time to Thy most Holy Name, the Father, and the Son, and the Holy Spirit, now, and always, even for ever and ever. Amen.

Peace be with you all. Bow your heads to the Lord.

Having attained our mutual desires, O Lord, and having consummated the rite of marriage as it was in Cana of Galilee, also in drawing the covenants concerning it to a close, we Thy servants, ascribe glory to Thee, the Father, and the Son, and the Holy Spirit, now, and always, even for ever and ever. Amen.

The priest then removes the crowns.

Advice

You will find that it is harder to focus and plan for future events after your wedding day. Consequently, the customs that take place during the reception are easier to implement than the ones that take place afterwards. If you are not leaving for your honeymoon right away, we recommend such postnuptial traditions as an "introduction" event, but so long as they are coordinated by someone else.

Our advice for most of the customs has already been given above, except for the following three:

THE LOVING CUP

The loving cup is filled with options. You could, for example, have a silver cup engraved with your names and your wedding date. The cup would then serve as a poignant memento of your wedding and could be used on anniversaries thereafter. You could also find a precious cup with the intention of making it a family heirloom. At one wedding we witnessed, the couple had put their loving cup (which had been in the bride's family for generations) on the top of the wedding cake instead of the usual plastic bride-and-groom figurines. It was a stunning success and the talk of the reception. The loving cup can also come in use when one is on a tight budget, acting as a tasteful substitute for the wedding cake itself (the cutting of which serves the same symbolic purpose). A more affordable dessert could then be served instead.

In any case, finding a simple, elegant silver or pewter chalice should not be too difficult. Antique stores, some of the finer department stores and Judaica shops (even if you are not Jewish) are good places to search. For internet searches, we suggest the search word "goblet" in addition to "cup," "loving," "silver," etc. Nuremberg bridal beakers and *quaiches* can be found in specialty catalogs or on the internet. From what we can tell, however, glass-bottom *quaiches* and French *coupes de marriage* are a rarity; a couple's best option is to use a solid *quaich* or a silver goblet. We should also mention that there is a French tradition in which the bride's godmother gives the cup as a gift to her goddaughter. This could be a good idea for the godmother who wishes to contribute meaningfully to the festivities.

When to use the loving cup will depend on what else is taking place during your reception. If you have a wedding cake, the cup should be used before the dinner; if you do not, it should be used after the dinner but before the dessert or whenever the best man's toast is given.

Finally, if your cup is an antique, remember to polish it a couple of days before the wedding, and don't forget to bring it to the reception!

THE BLESSING OF THE BREAD

As mentioned above, this custom can also substitute for the wedding cake at more modest receptions, and it is ideal for a couple that has no reception at all but wishes to leave for their honeymoon right after the service. A brief blessing of the bread in the sacristy of the church would be a simple yet meaningful replacement of the feast that would normally follow.

Couples eager to embrace their ethnic heritage at their wedding should inquire into whether that heritage includes special nuptial breads or fruitcakes. For example, a special braided bread is used for weddings in Crete, rye bread is used along with salt in Poland, *brudlaupskling* is used in Norway, an elaborately decorated bread called *korovai* is used in the Ukraine, bread and salt are ritually tasted in Russia, and so on. Fruit-cakes have also been a favorite among some nationalities. A fruitcake liberally soaked in rum is popular in the Caribbean, while the English once partook of a wedding fruitcake with a top tier — dubbed the "christening cake" — that would be saved for the baptism of the couple's first child. Finally, the Scottish and Irish would ritually break an oatcake or bannock over (not on!) the head of the bride as she crossed the threshold of her new home after they had enjoyed a fruitcake laced with bourbon or brandy at the reception.

WEDDING BROOMS

An entire industry specializing in wedding brooms — and well-represented on the internet — has swept the country in response to the demand for period-piece and custom-made brooms appropriate for the ceremony and permanent home display. These brooms remain faithful to the simple straw models of yesteryear yet incorporate motifs symbolic of weddings or African-American culture. Wedding brooms can range from $35 to $120 depending on maker and materials. Most broom makers can design anything according to your specifications. This is an excellent way of personalizing the tradition and of making the broom a topic of in-terest in your home for years to come. Of course, this can also be done by buying one of the less expensive wedding brooms and adding the per-sonal details (favorite colors, family keepsakes, etc.) yourself.

An even more independent approach is to make the broom yourself. This has the advantage of imitating one's ancestors who gathered loose pieces of straw from the fields and bound them to a wooden handle with a leather strap. One bride from Seattle, Alley Rutzel, did just that. On the night before her wedding, she and her mother scoured their family's wooded backyard for the right branch and then spent the rest of the evening talking about marriage and constructing the broom. "It became a bonding moment for us," she says.*

CONSUMMATION RITES

Blessing one's marriage bed may not be for everyone, but it will be of interest for those who want to run the full gamut of nuptial festivities and for those who would gladly welcome children into their lives. Ideally it should take place after the reception and before the marriage is consummated, but if necessity compels, you may have the blessing either before the service or the following day.

* Kemba J. Dunham, "Sweep of History Helps Propel a Boom in Keepsake Brooms," *Wall Street Journal,* October 15, 1999, p. A6.

VIII. *Putting It All Together*

Lovers, once married, deem their bond
Then perfect, scanning nought beyond
For love to do but to sustain
The spousal hour's delighted gain.

Coventry Paltmore,
"The Wedding Sermon"

T HE DIFFERENT JEWELS in this book are obviously of little use if they are not arranged properly in the right setting. Many parts do not make a whole, not even when each part is good in and of itself. And so, when crafting your "perfect bond," it is important to have all of its elements harmonize into one seamless celebration. Since this is no easy task (especially when a fusion of two different religious traditions is being attempted), we have dedicated this separate chapter to putting it all together. After a discussion on choosing the right time and place, we will present the three basic models available to those seeking a traditional wedding. Then, we will devote a special section to interdenominational or interfaith services. Finally, we will offer advice on how to prepare your own wedding program.

Time and Place

Though a host of different factors will play a role in determining the time and place of your wedding, one of them that should not be overlooked is the religious. Virtually all sacred traditions have conventions regarding the location and hour of weddings. While a number of these are not mandatory, they are nevertheless helpful to keep in mind when making your preparations.

CHRISTIAN

Christian customs generally follow the rhythm of the church calendar. Today in the Catholic Church, for example, a wedding can technically be held on any day of the year, but the Solemn Nuptial Blessing (see Chapter VI) cannot be given during Advent, Lent, and/or on Christmas Day or Easter Sunday. Moreover, during the penitential seasons of Advent and Lent it is not considered appropriate to have any ceremonies or flourishes that are too jubilant, such as flowers on the altar. Formerly in the Catholic and Anglican churches, and still in the Eastern Orthodox churches today, weddings were prohibited altogether during the Great Fast of Lent and on other specified fast days and feasts.

On the other hand, days which fall outside these periods have been considered particularly choiceworthy. The Irish, for example, considered Shrovetide (the three days prior to Lent) to be the luckiest time for a wedding, while the Italians, despite Church reluctance to have weddings on the Lord's day, consider Sunday the most auspicious.

As for place, virtually all Christian groups (except Christian Scientists) agree that marriage should ideally take place in a church. The reason for this near-unanimity varies from group to group, but the general consensus is that it is appropriate for something which is to be hallowed in the sight of God to take place in a space consecrated to God. This rule, however, is not iron-clad: The longstanding Protestant tradition in America of garden weddings is a case in point. As for time, the traditional hours for a Christian wedding are from nine o'clock in the morning until noon (whence comes our Hollywood image of wedding parties in morning dress). This, too, however, has changed a great deal in recent years.

Jewish law is relatively indifferent about place, relatively strict about time. A wedding can be held almost anywhere deemed suitable (be it synagogue or home, indoors or outdoors), but it cannot be held on certain days. Chief among these is the Sabbath, for the obvious reason that work is required to put a wedding feast together. (A wedding can, however, be held an hour and a half after sunset on a Saturday night without violating this proscription.) Celebrating a wedding on a major holiday is also forbidden. Thus, weddings are not allowed on Rosh Hashanah, Yom Kippur, Passover, Shavuot, and Sukkot. Orthodox and Conservative Jews add to this list the two periods of public mourning: the three weeks which commemorate the destruction of the Temple (generally in July or August) and the seven weeks in April or May called the Omer period. The one exception is the thirty-third day in Omer — a popular day, incidentally, for weddings in the state of Israel.

As for days of the week, Wednesday was once the day for the marriage of a maiden and Thursday for the marriage of a widow. During the Middle Ages, it was considered bad luck to be married on Monday (because, according to Gen. 1:6-9, God had created the firmament on that day but did not call it "good"), while Friday was the most popular day. Today, Saturday night and Sunday are the most popular.

Finally, the traditional hour for a Jewish wedding is sometime between noon and early evening. Special preference is given to marrying on the new moon (the beginning of the Jewish month), especially when the moon is rising in the sky (as this symbolizes growth and fertility).

The Three Classics

In every genre there is a classic. It might not be the first of its kind, and it most certainly will not be the last, but the classic somehow distinguishes itself from its cousins to become the standard against which all others are measured. In the wedding annals of our society there are three such classics. The first is the ancient *chuppah* ceremony of Judaism, the second is the traditional Roman Catholic rite of marriage (from the so-called Tridentine rite), and the third is the service for the "solemnization of matrimony" from the 1790 Episcopalian *Book of Common Prayer*. In figuring out how to put it all together, we can think of no better way than to let one of these serve as your template.

But a note of caution before you begin. Consulting these classics is one thing; using them in their entirety is another. As we have mentioned before, most Christian churches significantly revised their marriage rites in the latter half of the twentieth century. The Episcopalian Church's *Book of Common Prayer*, for example, has undergone several revisions since 1790, while the Catholic rite of matrimony was substantially altered in 1969 along with the rest of the liturgy. Moreover, a number of the Protestant denominations that formerly drew from the 1790 *Book of Common Prayer* now have different marriage services.

This, however, should not be viewed as an insurmountable problem, as the recent rites have a good deal of latitude regarding sensible modification. The new Catholic ceremony, for example, makes allowance for "praiseworthy" customs and prayers not included in the new service, enabling couples to retrieve and incorporate time-honored elements. Most Protestant churches take a similar view. *The United Methodist Book of Worship* has a clause that is shared in spirit by many: "Ethnic and cultural traditions are encouraged and may be incorporated into the service at the discretion of the pastor."

Furthermore, many churches have stipulations that allow couples to celebrate their wedding in a more holistically traditional manner, and more and more are taking advantage of these provisions. The Presbyterian and Methodist books of worship have new "services of Christian marriage," but both include the traditional service as well. In the same vein the Catholic Church permits its faithful to celebrate their nuptials according to the classic Tridentine rite (or, as it is now called, the extraordinary form of the Roman rite).* Again, it is crucial to consult with your presider.

---

* "For [the] faithful and priests who request it, the pastor should allow celebrations in this extraordinary form for special circumstances such as marriages" (His Holiness Pope Benedict XVI, *Summorum Pontificum*, 7 July 2007, Art. 5, §3).

JEWISH

This centuries-old ceremony has a plethora of customs surrounding it which vary according to such factors as whether one is Sephardic or Ashkenazic, Reform or Orthodox, etc. The essence of the Jewish *chuppah*, however, is clearly laid out in Halakic law and is followed by all. What follows is an English translation of the core ceremony, together with some of the more popular traditional customs now making a come-back.

The veiling of the bride & the signing of the *Ketubah.* Before the wedding ceremony begins the groom can veil the bride himself in order to avoid being deceived like Jacob (who, because the bride was veiled, could not tell he was marrying Leah instead of Rachel). After the veiling, the groom and his two witnesses then sign the *ketubah* in an antecham-ber of the synagogue. The father's blessing can also take place immedi-ately prior to the signing (see Chapter V).

Procession While the cantor chants a psalm or the musicians play a march (see Chapter II), the wedding party proceeds to the *chuppah* in the following order:

> Bride's grandparents
> Groom's grandparents
> Bridesmaid and Groomsman
> Best Man
> Groom's Father, Groom, Groom's Mother
> Bridesmaid and Groomsman
> Maid of Honor
> Bride's Father, Bride, Bride's Mother

Circling It is customary (though not required) for the bride to circle the groom either before going under the *chuppah* or at some other point in the ceremony (see Circling, Chapter V).

Positions under the *Chuppah* The standard positions of the wedding party under the *chuppah* are as follows.

Rabbi

| Groom's | Groom | Bride | Bride's |

Groom's   Groom   Bride   Bride's
Mother & Father   Mother & Father
Best Man   Maid of Honor

The Ceremony Proper begins with the cantor or rabbi greeting the congregation:

> Welcome in the name of the Lord our God,
> Welcome in this house of the Lord our God.

The presider then invokes the blessing of God upon this wedding:

> Splendor is upon everything
> Blessing is upon everything
> Who is full of this abundance
> Bless this groom and bride.*

Before the first cup is drunk, the rabbi recites the three betrothal benedictions (birkat esurin):

> Blessed art Thou, O Lord our God, King of the universe, who hast created the fruit of the wine.

> Blessed art Thou, O Lord our God, King of the universe, who hast sanctified us with Thy commandments, and hast forbidden us fornication, and hast restrained us from the betrothed, but hast permitted us those who are married to us by means of the canopy and sacred rites.

> Blessed art Thou, O Lord, who sanctifiest Israel by means of the bridal canopy and sacred marriage rites.

The rabbi may or may not drink from the cup before the couple. The groom and then the bride now drink from the first cup.

---

* The translation of this particular blessing is by Debra Cash, found in Anita Diamant's *The New Jewish Wedding* (New York: Summit Books, 1985).

Next, the groom takes a ring of gold, shows it to the witnesses, and places it on the forefinger of her right hand. He then says to her in Hebrew and English:

Behold, with this ring thou art wedded to me, according to the law of Moses and Israel.

The rabbi now reads the ketubah *(see Chapter IV). The presider then presents it to the groom, who in turn presents it to the bride. (The bride later gives it to an attendant for safekeeping.) Afterwards the rabbi delivers a brief sermon, followed by a reading from Scripture. Passages from the Song of Solomon, such as the one which follows, are especially popular:*

Behold my beloved speaketh to me: "Arise, make haste, my love, my dove, my beautiful one, and come. For winter is past, the rain is over and gone. The flowers have appeared in our land, the time of pruning is come; the voice of the turtle is heard in our land. The fig tree hath put forth her green figs; the vines in flower yield their sweet smell. Arise, my love, my beautiful one, and come. My dove in the clefts of the rock, in the hollow places of the wall, shew me thy face, let thy voice sound in my ears. For thy voice is sweet, and thy face comely. . . ." My beloved is mine and I am his who feedeth among the lilies.

Following the reading the rabbi prays the seven nuptial benedictions (sheva b'rachot).

At this point, in accordance with Sephardic custom, parents may place a tallit on the heads of the bride and groom (see Chapter V):

Blessed art Thou, O Lord our God, King of the universe, who createst the fruit of the vine.

Blessed art Thou, O Lord our God, King of the universe, who hast created every thing for Thy glory.

Blessed art Thou, O Lord our God, King of the universe, who hast formed man.

Blessed art Thou, O Lord our God, King of the universe, who hast formed man after Thy image, in the image of the likeness of Thy form, to establish him an everlasting structure; blessed art Thou, O Lord, who formest man.

Oh, cause Thou the barren one [Jerusalem] to be glad and rejoice at the gathering of her children unto her speedily amidst joy; blessed art Thou, O Lord, who causest Zion to rejoice in her children.

O Lord, cause these loving friends to rejoice, as Thou once didst send joy unto Thy creatures, whom Thou hast formed in the garden of Eden of old; blessed art Thou, O Lord, who causest the bridegroom and bride to rejoice.

Blessed art Thou, O Lord our God, King of the universe, who hast created gladness and joy, bridegroom and bride, love and brotherhood, delight and pleasure, peace and friendship: speedily, O Lord our God, let there be heard in the cities of Judah and in the streets of Jerusalem the voice of mirth and voice of gladness, the voice of the bridegroom and the voice of the bride, the voice of the merriment of the bridegrooms at their nuptial feasts, and of youths from their musical entertainments; blessed art Thou, O Lord, who causest them to prosper. "O give thanks to the Lord, for He is good; for His mercy endureth for ever." May joys increase in Israel, and sighs flee away.

After the blessing, the rabbi concludes:

By the power invested in me by the state of _____ and according to the law of Moses and Israel, I now pronounce you man and wife.

The groom takes a glass wrapped in cloth and smashes it under his heel.

The congregation responds to the sound with an enthusiastic Mazel Tov!

ROMAN CATHOLIC (TRIDENTINE)

The traditional Roman Catholic wedding may begin with a bridal procession, although both bride and groom may also approach the altar together, as they did in former ages. (And the quiet moments beforehand are a good time for the father's blessing [see Chapter VI].) While the groom and his attendants wait near the altar rail or sanctuary, the flower girls, ring-bearers, and bridesmaids process up the aisle (in that order), followed by the bride and her father. When the bride and groom meet, they turn to face the altar and the rite of matrimony (which is in both Latin and English) begins. The priest opens with an allocution to the congregation and couple, such as the French allocution given in Chapter III.

After the allocution the priest turns to the groom and asks:

N., wilt thou take N. here present for thy lawful wife, according to the rite of our Holy Mother the Church?

M.   I will.

He turns to the bride and asks:

N., wilt thou take N. here present for thy lawful husband, according to the rite of our Holy Mother the Church?

W.   I will.

The priest now has the groom and bride repeat after him:

M.   I, N.., take thee, N., for my lawful wife, to have and to hold, from this day forward, for better, for worse, for richer, for poorer, in sickness and in health, 'til death do us part.

W.   I, N.., take thee, N., for my lawful husband, to have and to hold, from this day forward, for better, for worse, for richer, for poorer, in sickness and in health, 'til death do us part.

The priest then says the following in Latin. As he does so, he may bind their joined hands with his stole, thus "tying the knot" (see Chapter V):

Ego conjúngo vos in matri-	I join you together in matri-
mónium. In nómine Patris et	mony. In the name of the Fa-
Fílii ✠ et Spíritus Sancti.	ther, and of the Son, ✠ and of
Amen.	the Holy Spirit. Amen.

The priest sprinkles the couple with holy water. Continuing in Latin, he now blesses the ring:

The ring ceremony follows.

V.	Adjutórium nostrum in nómine Dómini.	V.	Our help is in the name of the Lord.
R.	Qui fecit cælum et terram.	R.	Who made heaven and earth.
V.	Dómine, exáudi oratiónem meam.	V.	O Lord, hear my prayer.
R.	Et clamor meus ad te véniat.	R.	And let my cry come before Thee.
V.	Dóminus vobíscum.	V.	The Lord be with you.
R.	Et cum spíritu tuo.	R.	And with thy spirit.

The priest then says in Latin:

Orémus.	Let us pray.
Béne✠dic, Dómine, ánulum hunc, quem nos in tuo nómine bene✠dícimus: ut, quæ eum gestáverit, fidelitátem íntegram suo sponso tenens, in pace et voluntáte tua permáneat, atque in mútua caritáte semper vivat. Per Christum Dóminum nostrum.	Bless, ✠ O Lord, this ring, which we bless ✠ in Thy name: that she who is to wear it may render unbroken fidelity to her spouse. May she dwell in peace and in Thy will, and may she always live in mutual love. Through Christ our Lord.
R. Amen.	R. Amen.

The priest then sprinkles the ring(s) with holy water.

The groom now takes the ring, and putting it on the bride's finger, says:

With this ring I thee wed, and I plight unto thee my troth.

The groom may also follow the custom of invoking the Holy Trinity by placing the ring on the bride's index finger and saying, **In the name of the Father**, *on her middle finger and saying,* **And of the Son**, *and on her ring finger and saying,* **And of the Holy Spirit. Amen** *(see Chapter V).*

If there is a double-ring ceremony, the bride places her husband's ring on his finger, with the same words and in the same manner.

If coins are being given, they are blessed now with a blessing and with holy water (see Chapter V). After the exchanging of rings or coins, the priest then says in Latin:

In nómine Patris et Fílii ✠ et Spíritus Sancti. Amen.	In the name of the Father, and of the Son, ✠ and of the Holy Spirit. Amen.

The priest may continue in either English or Latin:

V.	Confírma hoc, Deus, quod operátus es in nobis.	V.	Confirm this, O God, what Thou hast wrought in us.
R.	A templo sancto tuo, quod est in Jerúsalem.	R.	From Thy holy temple, which is in Jerusalem.
V.	Kýrie, eléison.	V.	Lord, have mercy.
R.	Christe, eléison.	R.	Christ, have mercy.
V.	Kýrie, eléison.	V.	Lord, have mercy.

Pater Noster (said inaudibly until . . .)   Our Father (said inaudibly until . . .)

V.	Et ne nos indúcas in tentatiónem.	V.	And lead us not into temptation.
R.	Sed líbera nos a malo.	R.	But deliver us from evil.
V.	Salva fac servos tuos.	V.	Save Thy servants.
R.	Deus meus, sperántes in te.	R.	Who hope in Thee, my God.
V.	Mitte eis, Dómine, auxílium de sancto.	V.	Send them, O Lord, help from the sanctuary.
R.	Et de Sion tuére eos.	R.	And defend them out of Sion.

V. Esto eis, Dómine, turris fortitúdinis.	V. Be unto them, O Lord, a tower of strength.
R. A fácie inimíci	R. From the face of the enemy.
V. Dómine, exáudi oratiónem meam.	V. O Lord, hear my prayer.
R. Et clamor meus ad te véniat.	R. And let my cry come before Thee.
V. Dóminus vobíscum.	V. The Lord be with you.
R. Et cum spíritu tuo.	R. And with thy spirit.

The priest then says in either English or Latin:

Orémus. Réspice, quǽsumus, Dómine, super hos fámulos tuos: et institútis tuis, quibus propagatiónem humáni géneris ordinásti, benígnus assíste; ut qui te auctóre jungúntur, te auxiliánte servéntur. Per Christum Dóminum nostrum.	Let us pray: Look with favor, O Lord, we beseech Thee, upon these Thy servants, and graciously assist Thine institutions by which Thou hast ordained the propagation of the human race: that they who are yoked together by Thy authorship may be protected by Thy help. Through Christ our Lord.
R. Amen.	R. Amen.

In the Tridentine rite, the nuptial Mass now follows; but in the new Mass (in use since 1970), the rite of marriage generally takes places within the Mass, after the homily (see the new *Rites of the Catholic Church*). Either way, the Solemn Nuptial Blessing is given immediately after the consecration and the recitation of the "Our Father." It is at this point that a carecloth may be used (see Chapter V). Before the final blessing of the congregation, a second special nuptial blessing is also said. For both of these blessings, see Chapter V.

The conventions regarding the procession are the same as in the Catholic ceremony. The only difference is that in the Catholic service the father of the bride presents her to the groom as soon as they reach the altar rail, while in the Protestant service this is reserved for a special part in the ceremony.

> *At the day appointed for the Solemnization of Matrimony, the Persons to be married shall come into the Body of the Church, or shall be ready in some proper house, with their Friends and Neighbours; and standing there, the Man on the Right Hand, and the Woman on the Left, the Minister shall say,*

Dearly beloved, we are gathered together here in the sight of God, and in the face of this company, to join together this Man and this Woman in holy Matrimony, which is commended of St. Paul to be honourable among all men; and therefore it is not by any to be entered into unadvisedly or lightly; but reverently, discreetly, advisedly, soberly, and in the fear of God. Into this holy estate these two persons present now come to be joined. If any man can show just cause, why they may not lawfully be joined together, let him now speak, or else hereafter for ever hold his peace.

Editor's note: it is now allowable for scriptural readings to be added at this point (see Chapter III).

And also speaking unto the Persons who are to be married, he shall say,

I require and charge you both (as ye will answer at the dreadful day of judgment when the secrets of all hearts shall be disclosed),* that if either of you know any impediment, why ye may not be lawfully joined together in Matrimony, ye do now confess it. For be ye well assured, that if any persons are joined together otherwise than as God's word doth allow, their marriage is not lawful.

The Minister, if he shall have reason to doubt of the lawfulness of the

---

* The statement in parentheses was omitted after 1845.

proposed Marriage, may demand sufficient surety for his indemnification: but if no impediment shall be alleged, or suspected, the Minister shall say to the Man,

N., wilt thou have this Woman to thy wedded Wife, to live together after God's ordinance in the holy estate of Matrimony? Wilt thou love her, comfort her, honour, and keep her in sickness and in health; and, forsaking all others, keep thee only unto her, so long as ye both shall live?

The Man shall answer,

I will.

Then shall the Minister say unto the Woman,

N., wilt thou have this Man to thy wedded Husband, to live together after God's ordinance in the holy estate of Matrimony? Wilt thou obey him, and serve him, love, honour, and keep him in sickness and in health: and, forsaking all others, keep thee only unto him, so long as ye both shall live?

The Woman shall answer,

I will.

Then shall the Minister say,

Who giveth this Woman to be married to this Man?

Then shall they give their Troth to each other in this manner.

The Minister, receiving the Woman at her Father's or Friend's hands, shall cause the Man with his Right Hand to take the Woman by her Right Hand, and to say after him as followeth.

I, N., take thee, N., to my wedded Wife, to have and to hold, from this day forward, for better, for worse, for richer, for poorer, in sickness, and in health, to love and to cherish, till death us do part, according to God's holy ordinance, and thereto I plight thee my Troth.

Then shall they loose their Hands; and the Woman with her Right Hand taking the Man by his Right Hand, shall likewise say after the Minister:

I, N., take thee, N., to my wedded Husband, to have and to hold, from this day forward, for better, for worse, for richer, for poorer, in sickness, and in health, to love, cherish, and to obey, till death us do part, according to God's holy ordinance, and thereto I give thee my Troth.

Then shall they again loose their Hands; and the Man shall give unto the Woman a Ring. And the Minister taking the Ring shall deliver it unto the Man, to put it upon the fourth finger of the Woman's Left Hand. And the Man holding the Ring there, and taught by the Minister, shall say,

With this Ring I thee wed, and with all my worldly goods I thee endow: In the name of the Father and of the Son and of the Holy Ghost. Amen.

Then, the Man leaving the Ring upon the fourth finger of the Woman's Left Hand, the Minister shall say,

Let us pray.

Our Father. . . . But deliver us not from evil. Amen.

O eternal God, Creator and Preserver of mankind, Giver of all spiritual grace, the Author of everlasting life: Send Thy blessing upon these Thy servants, this man and this woman, whom we bless in Thy Name; that, as Isaac and Rebecca lived faithfully together, so these persons may surely perform and keep the vow and covenant betwixt them made (whereof this Ring given and received is a token and pledge), and may ever remain in perfect love and peace together, and live according to Thy laws, through Jesus Christ our Lord. Amen.

Then shall the Minister join their Right Hands together, and say,

Those whom God hath joined together, let no man put asunder.

Editor's Note: when the minister joins their hands, he may at this time wrap them with his stole, thus "tying the knot" (see Chapter V).

Then shall the Minister speak unto the Company:

Forasmuch as N. and N. have consented together in holy Wedlock, and have witnessed the same before God and this company, and thereto have given and pledged their troth, each to the other, and have declared the same by giving and receiving a Ring, and by joining hands; I pronounce that they are Man and Wife. In the name of the Father, and of the Son, and of the Holy Ghost. Amen.

And the Minister shall add this Blessing:

God the Father, God the Son, God the Holy Ghost, bless, preserve, and keep you; The Lord mercifully with His favour look upon you, and fill you with all spiritual benediction and grace; that ye may so live together in this life, that in the world to come ye may have life everlasting. Amen.

Interdenominational and Interfaith Weddings

When two people not belonging to the same faith wish to marry, it is natural for them to want to incorporate something of their own religious tradition into the wedding. "Mixed weddings" (as they are called) can be easy to do or they can be difficult — it all depends on the *mores* of the religious community. *Halaka* (the Jewish legal tradition), for example, prohibits any marriage between Gentile and Jew, a fact which makes preparation for such a wedding rather difficult.

What follows are a number of mixed arrangements and our tentative suggestions for them. Remember, however, that the rules of your own religious community or presider should take complete precedent over anything stated below. Some religious communities have clearly defined parameters for mixed weddings with which our generic advice may not be compatible. Early consultation with your presider will enable you to know what those parameters are.

PROTESTANTS OF DIFFERENT DENOMINATIONS

The intermarriage of Protestants does not present any great liturgical difficulties for one simple reason to which we have alluded several times already: The weddings in a number of American denominations are traditionally based on the 1790 *Book of Common Prayer.* The couple can therefore meet on this common ground even if neither is an Episcopalian. If, on the other hand, your denominations have moved away from the old *Book of Common Prayer,* chances are they have actually moved closer to each other liturgically. The Ecumenical Liturgy put out by the "Consultation on Common Texts" in 1987, for example, so embodies the commonalities of contemporary Protestant wedding liturgies that it has been endorsed by a large number of U.S. churches.

We should also mention that recent renewals of interest in the value of religious ceremony and symbol should enable you to incorporate various customs, such as the presentation of a Family Bible, into your wedding (see Chapter V).

PROTESTANT/CATHOLIC

The wedding of a Catholic and a non-Catholic by a Roman Catholic priest would traditionally be a toned-down affair. Mass would not be offered, the blessing of the ring or the nuptial blessing would not be given, and the actual rite of marriage would be significantly abridged.* This in itself makes the ceremony closer in appearance to a traditional Protestant wedding and should therefore be more gratifying to the Protestant bride or groom and his or her family. The Catholic Church's latest guidelines on such marriages should make this easy to facilitate.

If, on the other hand, a Catholic is being married in a Protestant wedding, a number of Catholic prayers and blessings can be added to the

---

* Since the Second Vatican Council, these laws have been relaxed, but most priests still recommend a wedding ceremony without a Mass in the case of a mixed marriage. This is seen as a more welcoming gesture to the non-Catholic party and his or her family, since there will be no Holy Communion from which they are excluded.

service, and so can more music, since Catholics are accustomed to longer wedding ceremonies. Thus, to the 1790 rite a blessing of the ring can be added along with, say, a final blessing from the Middle Ages. One could also include customs more associated with Catholicism, such as the coins or the carecloth, even though neither is, strictly speaking, exclusively Catholic.

JEWISH/GENTILE

There is a consistent logic to the Jewish prohibition against intermarriage. According to the Jewish tradition, the essence of Jewish marriage is the mutual pledge of bride and groom to live "according to the law of Moses and Israel." Since a Gentile lives by neither, he or she could never make this pledge. It is for this reason that not only is an authentic Jewish wedding impossible, strictly speaking, for a mixed couple, but even getting a rabbi to preside at such a wedding is enormously difficult. The rabbis who preside at a mixed wedding (even though the marriage will still have no standing in Jewish law) usually require several pre-nuptial meetings and often request an agreement from the Gentile partner to raise the children in the Jewish tradition. (Other conditions, such as membership in the congregation, may also apply.) Couples should also be cautious of so-called "mercenary" rabbis who demand a hefty fee for providing their services. Having a wedding presided over by representatives of both faiths is unlikely, as rabbis rarely preside alongside clergy from another confession (and there are a number of Christian clergy that are not fond of the arrangement either). Finally, it should be kept in mind that depending on the area, having a synagogue wedding is far more problematic than finding a rabbi or cantor to officiate outside the synagogue.

Catholic/Jewish

If, however, your mixed wedding is to be presided over by a Catholic priest, it is possible to infuse the basic Catholic rite with those customs that most closely bespeak Catholicism's roots in Judaism. For example,

Psalm 45 could be used at some point, along with a reading from the Song of Solomon or the Book of the Prophet Hosea. At the wedding reception, a number of Jewish customs and prayers may be incorporated, including the Grace after the Meal and the Seven Nuptial Blessings (see Chapter VII). Also, a loving cup, either in its Christian or Jewish form, can be used (ibid.).

Protestant/Jewish

For the marriage of a Protestant and a Jew, we recommend following the same principles involved in the marriage of a Catholic and a Jew.

Wedding Programs

As we mentioned in the general introduction, wedding programs enlighten your guests and provide them a lasting keepsake of the day. Whether your program is synoptic (covering only the main parts of the service) or comprehensive, it is the perfect way to inform your guests of what to expect and to satisfy their curiosity about your musical or scriptural selections. Wedding programs are especially important if your service is in another language, such as Hebrew or Latin, since they enable all of your guests to appreciate the service regardless of their knowledge of your religious tradition. And they are the perfect vehicle for explaining any unusual customs you have included.

SYNOPTIC PROGRAMS

In most cases a brief synopsis of your wedding in a four-page booklet is all that is necessary to ensure that your guests are duly enlightened. Synoptic programs generally give the names of the service's participants, its music and readings, and each of its principal parts. Special explanations or instructions (e.g., "no photography") can also be included. Finally, the cover page can be adorned with a special symbol or a favorite citation on the meaning of marriage, while the back page can include a note of gratitude to parents, etc., instructions on the festivities to follow, or the bride and groom's new address.

The four-page booklet is the most popular kind of wedding program, but for those who desire even greater simplicity, a single 8½" × 11" piece of paper can include the same information without the same cost or amount of preparation. Like booklets, single-page programs can also be done beautifully, especially when sufficient thought regarding the right combination of font, stationery, or ribbon is invested into them.

Protestant

The following is an example of a simple, four-page Protestant wedding booklet as it would appear on a single sheet of (not yet) folded paper:

FIRST SIDE

page 4 (back)   *page 1 (cover)*

	The Marriage in Christ
	of
	Kristin Todd Mead
	and
	Charles Harold Barker, Jr.
We wish to express our profound gratitude to our family and friends for celebrating this joyous event with us, to our parents for their untiring love, and to George Johnson for help in the preparation of this booklet.	*July 12, 2008*
All are warmly invited to continue this celebration at the Shortoak Country Club immediately following the service.	*Park Street Church*
	Boston
Directions can be found in the vestibule of the church.	
	What God hath joined, let no man put asunder.

page 2   *page 3*

THE WEDDING PARTY		THE CEREMONY

THE WEDDING PARTY

Minister	Reverend Joseph T. Clark
Organist	Genevieve E. Schmidt
Trumpeter	Lester Armstrong
Maid of Honor	Mary Ann Vincent
Bridesmaids	Isabelle Mead
	Susan Mead
	Jolene Verlich
Best Man	Alexander Helprin
Groomsmen	Matthew Toy
	John Cabot
	Kevin Woestman
Ushers	Justin Ryan
	Patrick Faber
Flower Girl	Emily Sylvester
Ringbearer	Kevin Ryan

Please, no photographs during the service.
Thank you.

THE CEREMONY

PRELUDE
"Jesu, Joy of Man's Desiring," Bach

PROCESSIONAL
Trumpet Tune in D Major, Johnson

WELCOME

DECLARATION OF CONSENT

GIVING OF THE BRIDE

SCRIPTURE READING
Psalm 128

HYMN
"Praise to the Lord," Neander
(No. 43 in the blue hymnal)

SCRIPTURE READING
John 2:1-11

HOMILY

EXCHANGE OF VOWS AND RINGS

PRONOUNCEMENT OF MARRIAGE

BENEDICTION

RECESSIONAL
Trumpet Voluntary, Stanley

Catholic

A four-page booklet is also a convenient and suitable format for a Catholic wedding program, though since Mass is usually said in conjunction with the rite of marriage, there is bound to be more information on it. Also, because of changes to the liturgy after Vatican II, there are now two distinct ways to celebrate the sacrament of marriage. Hence, we include two examples of what pages two and three might look like. The first example follows the pre–Vatican II or Tridentine format of having the Mass after the rite of marriage, while the second follows the contemporary format of inserting the rite of marriage into the middle of the Mass. Both are presented here as they would appear on a single sheet of (not yet) folded paper.

FIRST SIDE

Traditional & Contemporary Catholic

page 4 (back)   *page 1 (cover)*

We wish to express our profound gratitude to our family and friends for celebrating this joyous event with us, to our parents for their untiring love, and to George Johnson for help in the preparation of this booklet. *All are warmly invited to continue this celebration at the Shortoak Country Club immediately following the service.* *Directions can be found in the vestibule of the church.*	*The Nuptial Mass* *Uniting* *Margaret Mary O'Brien* *and* *James Arthur Gonzales* *in the* *Sacrament* *of* *Holy Matrimony* *In the Year of Our Lord* *October 11, 2008* *St. Athanasius Church* *Boston* *And the two shall become one flesh . . .*

Second Side
Traditional (Tridentine) Catholic:

<table>
<tr><td>page 2</td><td>page 3</td></tr>
</table>

Wedding Party

Celebrant	Reverend Joseph T. Clark
Servers	Jonathan David
	Michael Nolan
Maid of Honor	Mary Ann Vincent
Bridesmaids	Isabelle O'Brien
	Susan Mead
	Jolene Verlich
Best Man	Alexander Helprin
Groomsmen	Matthew Toy
	John Cabot
	Tino Silva
Ushers	Justin Ryan
	Patrick Faber
Flower Girl	Emily Sylvester
Ringbearer	Bob Ryan
Organist	Genevieve E. Schmidt
Trumpeter	Lester Armstrong
Choir	Voces Seraphim,
	Richard Sezinsky, *Director*

The Rite of Marriage

Prelude: "Jesu, Joy of Man's Desiring," Bach
Mothers' Entrance: "Salve Mater," anon.
Processional: Trumpet Tune, Johnson

Opening Allocution: Paris Ritual, 1839
Declaration of Consent
Exchange of Vows: Cambrai, 1300s
Pronouncement of Marriage
Blessing and Exchange of Rings
Blessing and Endowment of Coins
   The custom of giving coins dates back to the days of Abraham and Isaac and signifies the husband's obligation to provide for his family and the wife's obligation to manage the household funds responsibly.

Benediction

The Nuptial Mass

Introit: Ps. 127:1,* Tob. 7:15
Kyrie: Missa Papae Marcelli, Palestrina
Gloria: Missa Papae Marcelli, Palestrina†
Epistle: Eph. 5:22-33
Graduale: Ps. 127
Gospel: Matt. 19:3-6
Offertory: Ps. 30:15,16
Solemn Nuptial Blessing & Carecloth
   Accompanying the most important nuptial blessing a Catholic couple can receive is the carecloth, an ancient symbol of the dignity and responsibilities of marriage, and of the graces which come from this sacrament.

Sanctus Dei: Missa Papae Marcelli, Palestrina
Agnus Dei: Missa Papae Marcelli, Palestrina
Communion: "Ave Verum Corpus," Mozart
Recessional: Trumpet Voluntary, Stanley

* Note: On the numbering of Psalm 128 (127), see the footnote on p. 29.
† Another difference between the ordinary (post–Vatican II) and extraordinary (traditional) forms of the Roman rite is that the former has an optional "Glory to God in the highest" while the latter, since it is a votive Mass for a non-grave matter, does not.

Contemporary Catholic:

page 2   *page 3*

WEDDING PARTY		THE NUPTIAL MASS & RITE OF MARRIAGE
Celebrant	Reverend Joseph T. Clark	Prelude: "Jesu, Joy of Man's Desiring," Bach
Servers	Jonathan David	Mothers' Entrance: "Salve Mater," anon.
	Michael Nolan	Processional: Trumpet Tune, Johnson
Maid of Honor	Mary Ann Vincent	Welcome
Bridesmaids	Isabelle O'Brien	Kyrie: Missa P. Marcelli, Palestrina
	Susan Mead	Epistle: Eph. 5:22-33
	Jolene Verlich	Responsorial Psalm: Ps. 127
		Gospel: Matt. 19:3-6
Best Man	Alexander Helprin	Homily: Paris Ritual, 1839
Groomsmen	Matthew Toy	Declaration of Consent
	John Cabot	Exchange of Vows: Cambrai, 1300s
	Tino Silva	Pronouncement of Marriage
		Blessing and Exchange of Rings
Ushers	Justin Ryan	Blessing and Endowment of Coins
	Patrick Faber	*The custom of giving coins dates back to the days of Abraham and Isaac and signifies the husband's obligation to provide for his family and the wife's obligation to manage the household funds responsibly.*
Flower Girl	Emily Sylvester	Offertory: Ps. 30:15,16
Ringbearer	Bob Ryan	
		Solemn Nuptial Blessing & Carecloth
Organist	Genevieve E. Schmidt	*Accompanying the most important nuptial blessing a Catholic couple can receive is the carecloth, an ancient symbol of the dignity and responsibilities of marriage, and of the graces which come from this sacrament.*
Trumpeter	Lester Armstrong	
Choir	Voces Seraphim,	Agnus Dei: Missa P. Marcelli
	Richard Sezinsky, *Director*	Communion: "Ave Verum Corpus," Mozart
		Recessional: Trumpet Voluntary, Stanley

Jewish

Programs have not been a common feature of Jewish weddings, but this is changing somewhat as more couples with diverse sets of friends wish to provide some outline for their Gentile guests. This can be done either by simply naming the principal parts of the service, or by providing a brief commentary as well. We present here an example of the former, but a booklet of explanation would not be that much more difficult to do (see the Advice section at the end of this chapter). As always, we present the booklet as it would appear on a single sheet of (not yet) folded paper:

FIRST SIDE

page 4 (back)   *page 1 (cover)*

The Chuppah

of

Susannah Goldberg

and

Eric Schwartz

We wish to express our profound gratitude to our family and friends for celebrating this joyous event with us, to our parents for their untiring love, and to George Johnson for help in the preparation of this booklet.

May 11, 2008

6 Iyar 5768

All are warmly invited to continue our celebration at the Shortoak Country Club immediately following the service.

Beth Israel Synagogue

Boston

Directions can be found near the entrance to the synagogue.

I am my beloved's, and my beloved is mine.

WEDDING PARTY	**BEFORE THE CEREMONY**
Rabbi Joseph Eichenberg	The Veiling of the Bride: *Bedeken*
Cantor Dr. Seth Ingall	The Father's Blessing
	The Signing of the *Ketubah*
Best Man Mark Helprin	
Groomsmen Matthew Toy	**THE CEREMONY**
Jonathan Cabot	Processional: Psalm 45
David Winston	The Circling
	Welcome/Opening Blessing
Maid of Honor Mary Ann Vincent	The Betrothal Blessings *(Birkat esurin)*
Bridesmaids Isabelle Mead	Drinking of the First Cup
Susan Mead	(given by Ms. Judith Rosenberg)
Jolene Verlich	Giving of the Ring
	The Reading of the *Ketubah*
Chuppah Bearers Kevin Cohen	Sacred Reading: Song of Sol. 2:10-16
Joel Bernstein	The Nuptial Blessings *(Sheva b'rachot)*
Henry Lewittes	Drinking of the Second Cup
Michael Flame	Smashing of the First Cup
	At this point please enthusiastically respond, "Mazel Tov!"
	Recessional: "Siman Tov u'Mazel Tov,"
	("A Good Sign and Good Luck")
	AFTER THE CEREMONY
	Yichud (a quiet time for Susannah & Eric
	to be together alone)
Gentlemen, please wear a yarmulke while in the	
synagogue. These can be obtained near the entrance.	

COMPREHENSIVE PROGRAMS

Comprehensive programs, in which most or all of the service is transcribed verbatim, are necessary only when the service is held in another language. Due to their length we do not include any examples here, nor do we really need to, since the concept is self-explanatory. If you are making a comprehensive program, it is also a good idea to include brief explanations of some of the more unusual parts of the service.

Advice

The Service

Since we have discussed the general principles for putting together a wedding ceremony in the introduction and the advice sections at the end of each chapter, we will limit our remarks here to mixed weddings.

As a rule, elements from the same tradition harmonize better than those that come from different sources (obviously, customs and prayers shaped by the same theological and cultural worldview are inclined to be internally consistent). This does not mean that different religious customs are necessarily incompatible. Indeed, one of the things that a book like this makes clear is the striking similarity of all Western nuptial traditions. What it does mean, however, is that one should be on guard against any enthusiasm for the eclectic. Also, keep in mind that the reception provides an additional and in some ways better opportunity for self-expression.

Another concern with mixed weddings is the disposition of the presider and of one's family. Many couples, for example, are eager to please their parents by including as much of their family's faith in the service as possible. Sometimes, however, family members actually resent this as a "watering down" of their religion or as an unbearable syncretism of different creeds. If your only motivation in having an ecumenical wedding is maintaining good family relations, make sure first that it will have the desired effect.

Programs

A program can be professionally produced or, with the help of today's printers and personal computers, made at home. Making your own program is not difficult, but it can be time-consuming (do not be surprised when it takes longer than you had expected). It is therefore important to begin as early as possible.

That said, though an early start is preferable, it is also possible to be premature. Make sure that all of the details — such as time, place, and the names of the presider, musicians, and wedding party — are accurate and certain before you begin your final printing. A prudent move is to put everything in an electronic document as early as possible and then make changes as necessary.

The style of your program will depend on content and personal taste. We have seen single-page programs etched on ancient-looking parchment and rolled into a scroll, a circular leaflet with intricate spiral patterns on the cover, and a comprehensive booklet with Latin in one column and English in the other. Making your program a thing of beauty through thoughtful reflection on presentation and thorough attention to the smallest details — such as the right combination of font and stationery, or the perfect grade of paper — is a wise investment in time that you will not regret.

Making a booklet program on Microsoft Word   Open a new document. From the "File" menu, click "Page Setup." A window will appear, already on the "Margins" tab. Find "Multiple pages" about halfway down and change the box from "Normal" to "Book fold." This will automatically change the orientation of the paper from "Portrait" (vertical) to "Landscape" (horizontal); it will also print two pages per sheet and in the right order for a multi-page booklet. For example, for a four-page booklet it will print page four and page one on the first sheet and pages two and three on the second, in the order that we have shown above.

Before closing "Page Setup," adjust the margins for the amount of border space that you need. The "Gutter" feature, incidentally, provides more space along the fold to accommodate binding; it is generally not needed for smaller booklets with staples. Close "Page Setup" to begin typing your booklet.

For bilingual booklets, insert several two-columned tables with the help of the "Table" menu. Be forewarned that sometimes long tables do not carry over well onto the next page and that a second table will need to be created. Some people prefer working with the "Columns" feature (look for the icon on the menu bar), which inverts the two columns when they go over onto the next page.

Other advice: if you have a color printer, it is a nice touch to put the rubrics, or instructions, of your service in red (the word *rubric* actually comes from the Latin word for red). Second, if there is a part of the service where the presider makes the sign of the cross, it is useful (as we have done throughout *Wedding Rites*) to include the symbol ✠. This can be made from the Wingdings font by hitting Shift + X. For best results you may need to use a larger-sized font for it than for the rest of your text.

Finally, when making larger booklets (more than eight pages), some Microsoft users have found the "Book fold" function to be somewhat finicky. They prefer instead to change the orientation to Landscape and the Multiple Pages to "2 pages per sheet." Then, when they are done typing in the contents of the booklet and are ready to print, they change the Multiple Pages from "2 pages per sheet" to "Book fold."

Printing If you are using a duplex printer (a printer that prints on both sides of the paper automatically), select "Print," click on the "Properties" button, and select the appropriate options. According to Microsoft Help, "If you have a choice of setting the page orientation and duplex options, select landscape orientation, and flip the document on the short edge or short side."

If you are not using a duplex printer, you can simply print the entire document as you would any other. This will give you two pages on only one side of a sheet, but you can take these pages and copy them onto a single sheet of paper by using the 2→1 function on a photocopying machine. If you do not have a copy machine or are printing in color, you can instead open the "Print" dialog box and select "Manual Duplex" (on most versions this is below the "Properties" button). After Word has printed all of the pages on one side of the paper, it will prompt you to turn the stack over and feed the pages again. Be sure the print is facing the same direction as before so that half of the booklet's pages will not be upside down.

Binding A single-sheet, four-page booklet needs only to be folded neatly in half in order for it to be ready. On the other hand, for a more elegant alternative, one does not have to print both sides onto the same sheet of paper. One of the more beautiful booklets we have seen is from a couple who used white, speckled cardstock for the front and back cover, and a translucent vellum sheet for pages two and three inside.

The vellum was attached to the cover through a single hole by a colored ribbon.

Booklets larger than four pages can also be bound by ribbons and the like or by staples. Stapling is the easiest, though as most staplers do not extend a full five and a half inches, you may need to purchase a special "long reach" stapler at an office supply store.

APPENDIX A

Wedding Album Recordings

T HE FOLLOWING COMPACT DISCS are compilations of musical pieces traditionally used at weddings. We include them here as a convenient way to collect ideas and make decisions. And, to save time, we have assessed these albums according to precisely how useful they are. One bell (♤) means that the CD is in our opinion helpful, and two bells (♤♤) mean that it is in our opinion very helpful. Not all albums, of course, will be equally useful to everyone. Our recommendations for chant, polyphony, and choral music, for example, will not apply to all.

♤♤ 25 *Wedding Favorites.* Johann Sebastian Bach, Jeremiah Clarke, et al. Vox (Classical), 2000 (catalog no. 8848). This useful collection of recognizable classics ranges from organ pieces to choir and vocal by secular, Protestant, and Catholic composers.

♤ *Baroque for Brides to Be — a Musical Bouquet.* Johann Sebastian Bach, Handel, et al. PGD/Philips, 1997 (catalog no. 456355). This *mostly* baroque collection of twenty pieces focuses on the instrumental music used for processionals and recessionals.

♤ *Best-Loved Wedding Music.* Bach, Mendelssohn, et al. EMD/Seraphim-Blue, 1997 (catalog no. 69592). What is best-loved, of course, depends on the lover, but this collection of sixteen classical pieces does not do a bad job in presenting both popular and lesser known works.

♫ *The Best Traditional Wedding Music.* Chopin et al. St. Clair Records, 2001 (catalog no. 1051). While the "best" is an overstatement, this fourteen-track CD deserves credit for a distinctive assembly of classical pieces, such as Fritz Kreisler's charming "Liebesfreud" and Chopin's Étude Op. 10.

Bride's Book. Jeremiah Clarke, Andre Campra, et al. Pro Arte, 1992 (catalog no. 564). A half-traditional, half-contemporary collection of seventeen pieces. Since our general rule of thumb is to eschew anything originally sung by Bette Midler, we must attach a *caveat emptor* to this CD.

♫ *Bride's Guide to Wedding Music.* Jeremiah Clarke, Johan Pachelbel, et al. EMD/Angel, 1993 (catalog no. 64899). A total of eighteen prelude, processional, ceremonial, and recessional compositions.

♫ *Bride's Guide to Wedding Music, Vol. 2.* Georg Frideric Handel, James Molloy, et al. EMD/Angel, 1998 (catalog no. 66817). This sequel to the popular collection above has the same advantage as the first volume, covering most musical aspects of the ceremony.

♫ *Ceremonial Music for Trumpet and Organ/Smedvig, Murray.* Marc-Antoine Charpentier, Henry Purcell, et al. Telarc, 1993 (catalog no. 80341). Seventeen more or less classical pieces performed with the instruments most used in weddings today.

♫ *Chant Gregorien/Alfred Deller, Deller Consort.* Traditional Anonymous. Musique d'Abord (Fr.), 1990 (catalog no. 190235). Contains "The Wedding of Cana," a superb set of Gregorian chants appropriate for a wedding ceremony.

♫ *Classical Wedding.* George Frederic Handel, Beethoven, et al. EMD/Chordant, 1996 (catalog no. 25353). Sixteen classical selections, including Albert Hay Malotte's "The Lord's Prayer."

Classical Wedding, Vol. 2. Jean Joseph Mouret, Bach, et al. EMD/Chordant, 1998 (catalog no. 25448). A sequel of twenty-three selections that contains some overlap with the original.

♫ *Classical Wedding Traditions.* Bach, Beethoven, et al. New Traditions, 2000 (catalog no. 7003). These sixteen compositions range from Mendelssohn's and Wagner's orchestral bridal marches to the English folk song "Greensleeves" on harp.

The Classic Wedding Album/Domingo, Terfel, Te Kanawa, et al. Johann Sebastian Bach et al. PGD/Deutsche Grammophon, 1999 (catalog no. 445478). A comprehensive coverage of all musical parts of the ceremony that is unfortunately marred by the inclusion of Broadway tunes.

The Complete Wedding Album — There Is Love. André Campra, Bach, et al. Telarc, 1998 (catalog no. 80490). A two-CD set of thirty-five selections of mixed quality.

A Day to Remember — Instrumental Music for Your Wedding Day. O'Neill Brothers. O'Neill Brothers, 2004 (catalog no. 1208). Bach and Beethoven together with Shania Twain and Kenny G? That is a day to remember — or to try to forget.

Enhanced CD — Wedding Day. Johann Pachelbel et al. Platinum Distribution, 1996 (catalog no. 3544). We're not sure what is "enhanced" about this meager selection of thirteen pieces, half of which are not fit for the reception, let alone the ceremony.

🔔 *Firenze, 1539 — Music for the Wedding of the Duke of Florence.* Francesco Corteccia, Costanza Festa, et al. Tactus (It.), 1996 (catalog no. 530001). Contains beautiful polyphony composed for a royal Renaissance wedding.

🔔 *For Weddings/Kevin Bowyer.* Richard Wagner, Bach, et al. Nimbus, 1996 (catalog no. 7712). Contains twenty-three more or less well-known selections on a single CD.

🔔 *Greatest Hits — the Wedding Album.* Richard Wagner, Mendelssohn, et al. BMG/RCA, 1998 (catalog no. 63153). Despite the Top-40 title, a solid collection of twenty traditional pieces.

Heart Beats: Now & Forever — Timeless Wedding Songs. Various artists. Rhino/Wea, 1999 (catalog no. 75610). When songs by Chaka Khan and Bread are deemed "timeless," it is time to finally cancel one's subscription to pop culture.

Here Comes the Bride: Wedding Music. Virgil Fox (Organist). MCA Special Products, 1995 (catalog no. 20861). This low-priced CD of ten pieces is of special interest to those who will be using only an organist at their ceremony, but the selections are of mixed quality.

Jewish Wedding Album. Nancy Enslin, Deborah Benardot, performers. Platinum Distribution, 1994 (catalog no. 3478). An odd assortment of timeless classics and dated schmaltz.

♫ *The Knot Collection of Ceremony and Wedding Music Selected by the Knot's Carley Roney.* Sony, 2006 (catalog no. 92826). The editor-in-chief of *The Knot*, a bridal magazine, has chosen twenty-three reliable compositions from the less known to the well-trodden. Yo-Yo Ma performs Bach's Orchestral Suite No. 3 in D major.

♫ *La Pellegrina — Music for the Wedding of Ferdinando De Medici and Christine de Lorraine, Princess of France, Florence 1589.* Emilio de Cavalieri, Cristofano Malvezzi, et al. Sony Music, 1998 (catalog no. 63362, 2 CDs). This musical spectacle, extravagant even by the standards of the Medicis, is for the wedding feast following the ceremony.

The Look of Love — Music for Your Wedding. Platinum Distribution, 1993 (catalog no. 3440). A mixed bag of classical and kitsch.

♫ *Majestic Marches/Hayman, Slovak Philharmonic Orchestra.* Richard Wagner, Saint-Saens, et al. Naxos, 1992 (catalog no. 550370). A low-priced collection of great marches, a minority of which can be adapted to a wedding.

Marches from the Classics. Franz Liszt, Verdi, et al. Vox Cameo Classics, 1993 (catalog no. 8767). Two of the twelve marches on this CD are specifically for weddings.

♫ *A Midsummer Night's Dream — a Classical Wedding Album.* Henry Purcell, Wagner. et al. BMG/RCA, 1998 (catalog no. 63182). More than Mendelssohn can be found on this collection of sixteen wedding favorites.

♫ *Music for a Wedding.* Richard Wagner, Schubert, et al. Allegretto, 1994 (catalog no. 8033). Perhaps the lowest-priced wedding CD on the market, featuring a few well-known pieces and several obscure ones.

♫♫ *Music for Your Wedding — a Complete Guide.* Bach, Mozart, et al. Priory Records (UK), 1998 (catalog no. 644). This astonishing collection of thirty-two pieces on a single CD comes mighty close to fulfilling its title, and it is the only album we have seen that includes nuptial hymns as well as secular marches.

New Wedding Traditions, Vols. 1 and 2. Mikki Viereck and various. New Traditions, 2000 and 1999, resp. (catalog nos. 7001 and 7002). It has been decades since the phrase "gag me with a spoon" has come to our minds.

♫♫ *The #1 Wedding Album.* Bach, Charpentier, et al. Decca, 2003 (catalog no. 000027402). While the self-conferred honor of "number one" is a bit bombastic, this collection of thirty-eight traditional compositions on 2 CDs, performed on organ, trumpet, and orchestra, is well arranged and well selected.

O Perfect Love and Other Wedding Songs/Nancy Enslin. Johann Pachelbel, Bach, et al. Platinum Distribution, 1994 (catalog no. 3477). Twenty-six selections ranging from the sublime to the saccharine.

♫ *Orthodox Wedding Ceremony and New-Year Service/Popsavov.* Gega (Bulg.), 1997 (catalog no. 142). A must-have for anyone planning a Slavic Orthodox or Byzantine Catholic service.

♫ *Oxford Book of Wedding Music/Jeremy D. Filsell.* John Stanley, Mendelssohn, et al. Guild (UK), 1995 (catalog no. 7107). A solid collection of twenty-two traditional wedding favorites.

♫ *Roman: Music for a Royal Wedding/Halstead, Uppsala CO.* Johan Helmich Roman (Composer). Naxos, 1998 (catalog no. 8553733). A beautiful series of vocal and orchestral pieces from a seventeenth-century Swedish composer.

♫♫ *The Ultimate Wedding Album.* Johann Sebastian Bach, Handel, et al. PGD/London Classics, 1995 (catalog no. 48004). Like the *Complete Guide* listed above, this collection of nineteen pieces contains music for the ceremony proper as well as for the processional and recessional.

♫ *Volume 1 — Wedding Music.* Campra, Stanley, et al. Compose, 1995 (catalog no. 9948). This low-priced two-CD set contains thirty-two pieces of varying quality and renown.

🔔 *The Wedding Album — the Ultimate Collection of Nuptial Music*. Marc-Antoine Charpentier, Louis Vierne, et al. Wea/Atlantic/Erato, 1996 (catalog no. 99709). "Ultimate" is a bit of an exaggeration for this collection of sixteen classical pieces.

🔔 *The Wedding Album/Anthony Newman*. Felix Mendelssohn, Clarke, et al. Sony Music, 1991 (catalog no. 427273). An interesting assortment of twenty-eight more or less well-known pieces on a single CD.

Wedding Celebrations/Bogár, Budapest Strauss Ensemble. Naxos, 1994 (catalog no. 550900). Polkas and the like for the reception.

Wedding Gifts — Bach: Wedding Cantatas/Heidi Grant Murphy. Johann Sebastian Bach. Arabesque, 1997 (catalog no. 6690). A full serving of Bach's wedding cantatas.

🔔🔔 *Wedding Motets/Manfred Cordes, Weser-Renaissance*. CPO, 1997 (catalog no. 999396). For those with a choir and orchestra at their disposal, this is a good source for material.

🔔 *Wedding Music — Vivaldi, Bach, Purcell, Handel, Wagner, etc*. Antonio Vivaldi, Bach, et al. WEA/Atlantic/Erato, 1993 (catalog no. 92968). Nineteen prelude, processional, and recessional classics.

🔔 *Wedding Music/Bogár, Hock, Geiger*. Felix Mendelssohn et al. Naxos, 1994 (catalog no. 550790). A rather distinctive collection of sixteen wedding classics, including a waltz by Strauss and Schubert's popular "Ave Maria," which has been surprisingly underrepresented on the CDs we have seen.

🔔 *The Wedding Music Collection Vol 1/Hamrick, et al*. Virtuosi, 1998 (catalog no. 10393). Fifteen nuptial classics.

APPENDIX B

The Language of Flowers and Color

An exquisite invention this,
Worthy of love's most honeyed kiss,
This art of writing billet doux
In buds and odors, and bright hues;
In saying all one feels and thinks
In clever daffodils and pinks,
Uttering (as well as silence may)
The sweetest words the sweetest way.

Leigh Hunt,
"Love Letters Made of Flowers"

Flower	Meaning
Almond blossom	Hope
Amaryllis	Splendid beauty
Apple blossom	Preference
Asclepias (Swallow-wort)	Cure for heartache
Azalea	Temperance, Generous love
Basil	Good wishes
Bittersweet	Truth
Calla aethiopica	Feminine modesty
Carnation	Pure love
Daffodil	Chivalry
Dahlia	Forever yours
Daisy	Innocence
Forget-me-not	Forget me not
Heliotrope	Intoxicated devotion
Honeysuckle	Bond of love
Hyacinth	Love and games
Ivy	Fidelity, Marriage
Jasmine	Grace and eloquence
Jonquil	Desire
Laurel	Glory, Triumph
Lilac	First emotion of love
Lily	Purity
Lily of the Valley	Delicacy, Purity
Linden	Conjugal love
Mint	Virtue
Monk's Hood	Knight errantry
Myrtle	Love
Olive	Peace
Orange blossom	Chastity, Purity
Primrose	Hope, First flower

Flower	Meaning
Rose	Beauty
deep pink	Admiration
orange	Enthusiasm, Desire
pink	You are lovely
red	I love you, Courage, Desire
white	You are heavenly, Innocence, Purity
yellow	Joy, Gladness
Rosebud	Young girl
Rosemary	Fidelity
Star of Bethlehem	Purity
Stock	Lasting beauty
Sweet Pea	Delicate pleasure
Tulip	Honesty
Veronica	Fidelity, Saintliness
Violet	Modesty

Color	Meaning
Blue	Purity, The sublime or heavenly
Gold	Same as White
Green	Hope
Purple	Royalty (and in some contexts, Sorrow)
Red, Scarlet	Passion
White	Purity, Innocence, Rebirth

APPENDIX C

Scripture Readings for the
New Catholic Rite of Marriage

IN 1962, the Second Vatican Council called for revisions to the
Catholic rite of matrimony and the Solemn Nuptial Blessing. These
changes, prepared by a special "Consilium" after the Council ended,
were officially promulgated in 1969. The new rite contains many optional
parts: We include here the numerous official options now available for
Scripture readings. Other possibilities, such as different formulas for the
exchange of rings, the revised Solemn Nuptial Blessing, and the blessings
that may be used instead of it, can be found in *The Rites of the Catholic
Church*.

Scripture Readings

In the wedding Mass and in marriages celebrated without Mass, the following selections may be used:

1. OLD TESTAMENT READINGS

- Genesis 1:26-28, 31a
  Male and female he created them.

- Genesis 2:18-24
  The two of them become one body.

- Genesis 24:48-51, 58-67
  In his love for Rebekah, Isaac found solace after the death of his mother.

- Tobit 7:6-14
  May the Lord of heaven prosper you both. May he grant you mercy and peace.

- Tobit 8:4b-8
  Allow us to live together to a happy old age.

- Proverbs 31:10-13, 19-20, 30-31
  The woman who fears the LORD is to be praised.

- Song of Songs. 2:8-10, 14, 16a; 8:6-7a
  Stern as death is love.

- Sirach 26:1-4, 13-16
  Like the sun rising in the LORD's heavens, the beauty of a virtuous wife is the radiance of her home.

- Jeremiah 31:31-32a, 33-34a
  I will make a new covenant with the house of Israel and the house of Judah.

2. NEW TESTAMENT READINGS

- Romans 8:31b-35, 37-39
  What will separate us from the love of Christ?

- Romans 12:1-2, 9-18 (long form) or Romans 12:1-2, 9-13 (short form)
  Offer your bodies as a living sacrifice, holy and pleasing to God.

- Romans 15:1b-3a, 5-7, 13
  Welcome one another as Christ welcomed you.

- 1 Corinthians 6:13c-15a, 17-20
  Your body is a temple of the Spirit.

- 1 Corinthians 12:31–13:8a
  If I do not have love, I gain nothing.

- Ephesians 5:2a, 21-33 (long form) or 5:2a, 25-32 (short form)
  This is a great mystery, but I speak in reference to Christ and the
  Church.

- Philippians 4:4-9
  The God of peace will be with you.

- Colossians 3:12-17
  And over all these put on love, that is, the bond of perfection.

- Hebrews 13:1-4a, 5-6b
  Let marriage be held in honor by all.

- 1 Peter 3:1-9
  Be of one mind, sympathetic, loving toward one another.

- 1 John 3:18-24
  Love in deed and in truth.

- 1 John 4:7-12
  God is love.

- Revelation 19:1, 5-9a
  Blessed are those who have been called to the wedding feast of the
  Lamb.

3. Responsorial Psalms

- Psalm 33:12 and 18, 20-21, 22
  (5b) The earth is full of the goodness of the Lord.

- Psalm 34:2-3, 4-5, 6-7, 8-9
  (2a) I will bless the Lord at all times.
  Or: (9a) Taste and see the goodness of the Lord.

- Psalm 103:1-2, 8 and 13, 17-18a
  (8a) The Lord is kind and merciful. Or:
  (17) The Lord's kindness is everlasting to those who fear him.

- Psalm 112:1bc-2, 3-4, 5-7a, 7b-8, 9
  (1) Blessed is the man who greatly delights in the Lord's commands.
  Or: Alleluia.

- Psalm 128:1-2, 3, 4-5
  (1a) Blessed are those who fear the Lord.
  Or: (4) See how the Lord blesses those who fear him.

- Psalm 145:8-9, 10 and 15, 17-18
  (9a) The Lord is compassionate toward all his works.

- Psalm 148:1-2, 3-4, 9-10, 11-13ab, 13c-14a
  (13a) Let all praise the name of the Lord.
  Or: Alleluia.

4. ALLELUIA VERSE AND VERSE BEFORE THE GOSPEL

- 1 John 4:7b
  Everyone who loves is begotten of God and knows God.

- 1 John 4:8b, 11
  God is love.
  If God loved us, we also must love one another.

- 1 John 4:12
  If we love one another,
  God remains in us
  and his love is brought to perfection in us.

- 1 John 4:16
  Whoever remains in love,
  remains in God and God in him.

5. Gospels

- Matthew 5:1-12a
  Rejoice and be glad, for your reward will be great in heaven.

- Matthew 5:13-16
  You are the light of the world.

- Matthew 7:21, 24-29 (long form) or 7:21, 24-25 (short form)
  A wise man built his house on rock.

- Matthew 19:3-6
  What God has united, man must not separate.

- Matthew 22:35-40
  This is the greatest and the first commandment. The second is like it.

- Mark 10:6-9
  They are no longer two, but one flesh.

- John 2:1-11
  Jesus did this as the beginning of his signs in Cana in Galilee.

- John 15:9-12
  Remain in my love.

- John 15:12-16
  This is my commandment: love one another.

- John 17:20-26 (long form) or 17:20-23 (short form)
  That they may be brought to perfection as one.

A Selected Bibliography of Works Consulted

Perry H. Biddle, Jr. *Abingdon Marriage Manual.* Nashville: Abingdon Press, 1974.

J. Foote Bingham. *Christian Marriage: The Ceremony, History, and Significance.* New York: E. P. Dutton & Co., 1900.

Christopher N. L. Brooke. *The Medieval Idea of Marriage.* Oxford: Oxford University Press, 1989.

John Calvin. *La forme des prières et chants ecclésiastiques.* 1542; Kassel: Bärenreiter, 1959.

Catholic Church. *Liber sacramentorum gellonensis.* Turnholti: Brepols, 1981.

————. *Missale Romanum.* New York: Benziger, 1962.

————. *Rituale Romanum.* Tournai: Desclée, 1898.

Catholic Church in the United States. *Collectio Rituum.* Milwaukee: Bruce Publishing Co., 1954.

Edithe Lea Chase and Capt. W. E. P. French, U.S.A. *Toasts for All Occasions.* New York: Barse & Hopkins, 1903.

Consultation on Common Texts. *A Christian Celebration of Marriage: An Ecumenical Liturgy.* Philadelphia: Fortress Press, 1987.

Alicia Correa, ed. *The Durham Collector.* London: Boydell Press, 1992.

Mary Murray Delaney. *Of Irish Ways.* New York: Kilkenny Press, 1985.

Alöis de Smet. *Betrothment and Marriage: A Canonical and Theological Treatise with Notices on History and Civil Law.* St. Louis, MO: B. Herder Book Co., 1912.

Anita Diamant. *The New Jewish Wedding.* New York: Summit Books, 1985.

F. C. Eeles. *Traditional Ceremonial and Customs Connected with the Scottish Liturgy.* London: Longmans, Green, and Co., 1910.

Marius Ferotin, ed. *Le Liber Ordinum.* Rome: CLV, 1996.

Adrian Fortescue and J. B. O'Connell. *The Ceremonies of the Roman Rite Described.* Westminster, MD: Newman Press, 1958.

Philip and Hanna Goodman, eds. *The Jewish Marriage Anthology.* Philadelphia: Jewish Publication Society of America, 1965.

Rev. H. N. Hutchinson. *Marriage Customs in Many Lands.* London: Seeley and Co., Ltd., 1897.

D. Hyacinthus-Ludovicus de Quelen, Archbishop of Paris, ed. *Rituale Parisiense.* Lutetiae Parisiorum, A. Le Clere et Soc. Typographi, 1839.

Inter-Lutheran Commission on Worship. *Lutheran Book of Worship.* Minneapolis: Augsburg Publishing House, 1978.

Cuthbert Johnson and Anthony Ward, eds. *Missale Parisiense anno 1738 publici iuris factum.* Rome: CLV-Edizioni Liturgiche, 1993.

William Keeling, ed. *Liturgiae Britannicae.* London: William Pickering, 1851.

J. Wickham Legg, ed. *The Westminster Missal.* London, 1891.

————. "Notes on the Marriage Service in the Book of Common Prayer, 1549." In *The Library of Liturgiology and Ecclesiology for English Readers,* ed. Vernon Staley, pp. 181-224. London: Alexander Moring, Ltd., 1905.

Mendell Lewittes. *Jewish Marriage.* Northvale, NJ: Jason Aronson Inc., 1994.

E. A. Lowe, ed. *The Bobbio Missal: A Gallican Mass-Book.* London: Boydell Press, 1991.

Martin Luther. *Luther's Works.* Vol. 53. Philadelphia: Fortress Press, 1965.

Ivor Ben McIvor. *Scottish Toasts.* New York: H. M. Caldwell Co., 1908.

Frederick R. McManus, ed. *Parish Ritual.* New York: Benziger, 1962.

J. B. Molin and P. Mutembe. *Le rituel du mariage en France du XIIe au XVIe siècle.* Paris: Beauchesne, 1974.

National Conference of Catholic Bishops. *The Book of Blessings.* Collegeville: Liturgical Press, 1990.

————. *The Rites of the Catholic Church.* Collegeville: Liturgical Press, 1987.

Charles Paris. *Marriage in XVIIth Century Catholicism.* Montreal: Bellarmin, 1975.

Presbyterian Church in the United States General Assembly. *The Book of*

Common Worship. Philadelphia: Presbyterian Board of Publication & Sabbath School Work, 1906.

————. *The Worshipbook*. Philadelphia: Westminster Press, 1972.

————. *Book of Common Worship*. Louisville: Westminster/John Knox Press, 1993.

Albert Schoenfelder. *Liturgische Bibliothek*. Paderborn: Verlag von Ferdinand Schoeningh, 1904.

Beverly Seaton. *The Language of Flowers: A History*. Charlottesville: University Press of Virginia, 1995.

Martine Segalen. *Amours et Mariages de l'Ancienne France*. Paris: Berger Levrault, 1981.

Charles W. Shields, for the Presbyterian Church in the United States. *The Book of Common Prayer*. New York: Anson D. F. Randolph & Co., 1847.

K. W. Stevenson. *Nuptial Blessings: A Study of Christian Marriage Rituals*. London: Alcuin Club, 1982.

K. W. Stevenson and Mark Searle. *Documents of the Marriage Liturgy*. Collegeville: Liturgical Press, 1992.

United Methodist Church. *The Book of Worship for Church and Home*. Nashville: United Methodist Publishing House, 1964, 1965.

————. *The United Methodist Book of Worship*. Nashville: United Methodist Publishing House, 1992.

United States Conference of Catholic Bishops. *Lectionary for Mass*. Washington, DC: Confraternity, 2001.

F. E. Warren. *The Liturgy and Ritual of the Ante-Nicene Church*. 2nd ed. London: Society for Promoting Christian Knowledge, 1912.

Philip T. Weller, trans. and ed. *The Roman Ritual: The Sacraments and Processions*. Vol. I. Milwaukee: Bruce Publishing Co., 1950.

James F. White. *John Wesley's Prayer Book*. Cleveland: OSL Publications, 1991.

————. *The Sacraments in Protestant Practice and Faith*. Nashville: Abingdon Press, 1999.

Lady Wilde. *Quaint Irish Customs and Superstitions*. Cork: Mercier, 1988.

Permissions

"A Wedding Toast" from THE MIND-READER, copyright © 1971 and renewed 1999 by Richard Wilbur, reprinted by permission of Harcourt, Inc.

Excerpts from the *Lectionary for Mass for use in the Dioceses of the United States* Copyright © 2001, 1998, 1997 and 1970 Confraternity of Christian Doctrine, Inc., Washington, DC. Used with permission. All rights reserved. No portion of this text may be reproduced without permission in writing from the copyright holder.

The English translations of the Titles of the Readings and some of the Psalm Responses (in Appendix C of this book) are from *Lectionary for Mass* © 1969, 1981, 1997, International Committee on English in the Liturgy, Inc. All rights reserved.

Translation of *tenaim* document from Mendell Lewittes' *Jewish Marriage: Rabbinic Law, Legend, and Custom* (Northvale, NJ: Jason Aronson Inc., 1994) by permission of Jason Aronson, an imprint of Rowman & Littlefield Publishers, Inc. All rights reserved.

Index

64, 92, 97, 102, 106-7, 117, 119, 123, 125, 129, 142

German, 17, 45-46, 53, 71, 117-18, 119, 129
Greek, 79, 100

Hispanic, 102. *See also* Argentinean, Chilean, Mexican, Puerto Rican, Venezuelan
Homilies. *See* Allocutions
Hungarian, 93

Irish, 27, 53, 103, 116, 124, 128-29, 133, 134, 137, 139-40, 143, 146
Italian, 146

Jewish, xii, 17-20, 26, 29, 33, 37, 56, 72-73, 74, 76-77, 81-82, 84, 87, 99, 101, 112-13, 128, 132, 135, 147, 149-52, 162-63, 169-70. *See also* Ashkenazic, Sephardic

Ketubah, 72-73, 74, 149, 151
Kirkin', 139-40
Kiss, 9, 13, 95, 97

Loving Cup, 81-83, 98, 101-2, 112, 128-29, 141-42
Lutheran, 21, 31, 45-46, 52, 68, 79, 86, 113

Marriage Bed. *See* Consummation Rites
Methodist, 21, 66, 86-87, 90, 148
Mexican, 78, 96, 99, 102, 106
Music, 25-36, 38-39

Nights of Tobias, 116
Norwegian, 101, 143. *See also* Scandinavian

Orthodox (Christian), xii, 22, 74, 79, 146. *See also* Byzantine
Orthodox (Jewish), xii, 147. *See also* Jewish

Polish, 143
Presbyterian, 21, 31, 66, 70-71, 90. *See also* Calvinist
Programs (Wedding), 5, 22, 126, 163-74
Protestant, xii, 3, 29, 68, 74, 86, 91, 98,

146, 148, 157-60, 161-63, 164-65. *See also* Anglican, Calvinist, Church of Scotland, Episcopalian, Lutheran, Methodist, Quaker, Presbyterian
Puerto Rican, 102

Quaker, 71

Ring, 8n., 13, 14-16, 18, 63, 84-91, 102
Readings. *See* Biblical Readings
Roman Catholic, 9, 13, 21, 31-32, 47-49, 49-52, 53-55, 65-66, 77-78, 79, 85-86, 88-89, 91, 96-97, 98, 107-9, 115-20, 137, 146, 148, 153-56, 161-63, 166-68, 184-88. *See also* Tridentine
Russian, 143. *See also* Slavic

Scandinavian, 37, 79, 101
Scottish, 27, 93, 128-29, 131, 133, 137, 139-40, 143
Sephardic, xii, 77, 149, 151
Sermons. *See* Allocutions
Slavic, 79, 83n., 100. *See also* Czech, Polish, Russian, Ukrainian
Society of Friends. *See* Quaker
Spanish, 93, 119, 124, 137
Swedish, 101. *See also* Scandinavian
Swiss, 79

Tenaim, 17-20
Toasts, 126, 130-35
Tridentine, 65-66, 85, 88-89, 107-9, 120, 153-56, 166-67
Tying the Knot, 12, 91

Ukrainian, 100, 143
Unity Candle, 97-98

Veil. *See* Bridal Veil
Venezuelan, 102
Vows, 7, 59-71, 73-74

Wedding Brooms, 136, 143-44
Wedding Veil. *See* Carecloth
Welsh, 37